MAKE it WORK!

STONE AGE
PEOPLE

Author: Keith Branigan
Consultant: Norah Moloney, Ph.D
The Institute of Archaeology, University College, London
Series creator: Andrew Haslam

TWO CAN™

PRINCETON ■ LONDON

Published in the United States and Canada by
Two-Can Publishing LLC
234 Nassau Street
Princeton, NJ 08542

www.two-canpublishing.com

© 2001, 1998 Two-Can Publishing

For information on Two-Can books and multimedia,
call 1-609-921-6700, fax 1-609-921-3349, or visit our Web site at
http://www.two-canpublishing.com

Author: Keith Branigan
Editor: Kate Graham
Art Directors: Carole Orbell, Jill Plank
Senior Designer: Gareth Dobson
Managing Editor: Christine Morley
Commissioned photography: Ray Moller
Picture research: Deborah Dorman, Lyndsey Price
Production: Joya Bart-Plange
Model-makers: Melanie Williams, Peter Griffiths, Paul Holzherr, Greg Shaw

'Two-Can' is a trademark of Two-Can Publishing.
Two-Can Publishing is a division of Zenith Entertainment Ltd,
43-45 Dorset Street, London W1H 4AB

hc   ISBN 1-58728-306-9
sc   ISBN 1-58728-302-6

hc   1 2 3 4 5 6 7 8 9 10 02 01 00
sc   1 2 3 4 5 6 7 8 9 10 02 01 00

With thanks to Twyford Church of England School and the models: Richard Dare, Adeline Borbbey, Lester Cotier,
Matthew Grant, Payal Lakhani, James Moller, Anthony Rumble, James Sayle, Fiona Shacklady, Robert T-M Blankson.

Printed in Hong Kong by Wing King Tong

Contents

Studying Stone Age life

All human beings need food and shelter to survive. They also have a system of beliefs that gives shape and meaning to their lives. From **prehistoric** times, people have created different ways of meeting these basic requirements. By studying Stone Age people, we learn how they used the resources around them to build shelters and find food, and how they developed a way of life that enabled them to survive.

▷ *This plaster mold of a skull was found in Jericho, Jordan. It has shell eyes and dates from 7000 B.C.*

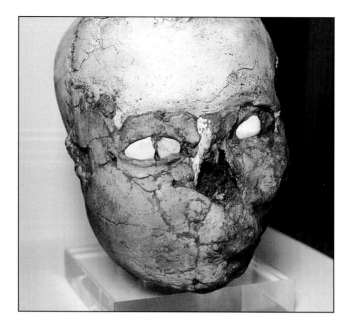

THE PERIOD OF TIME covered in this book is vast—about three million years! **Archaeologists** normally divide this time into three main periods: the **Paleolithic** (Old Stone Age), the **Mesolithic** (Middle Stone Age) and the **Neolithic** (New Stone Age).

THE PALEOLITHIC is such a long period of time (from three million B.C. to 10,000 B.C.) that it too is often divided up into Lower, Middle, and Upper phases.

THE MESOLITHIC began around 10,000 B.C., but ended at different times in different places. The Neolithic dates from about 8000 to 3000 B.C., but in some places it lasted longer. For example, in North America it continued until the arrival of the Europeans in the 1400's. Here, we have traced Stone Age people only down to about 3000 B.C.

To make things clearer, we have given symbols to the Lower/Middle Paleolithic, the Upper Paleolithic and the Mesolithic/Neolithic. These are used when the information relates to the time covered.

KEY FOR SYMBOLS

🐘 (mammoth)   **Lower/Middle Paleolithic** (3 million − 40,000 B.C.)

🏃 (spear-thrower)   **Upper Paleolithic** (40,000 − 10,000 B.C.)

🌾 (wheat grain)   **Mesolithic/Neolithic** (10,000 − 3000 B.C.)

WRITING HAD BARELY BEEN INVENTED by 3000 B.C., so we have to rely on objects we find to try and piece together what may have happened in the ancient past. As a result, we are never sure how Stone Age people lived, and experts often interpret the evidence very differently!

◁ *Female figurines may have been used by Stone Age people as symbols of fertility.*

ARCHAEOLOGISTS have the task of finding, digging up, and trying to understand the evidence of Stone Age people, the world in which they lived, and their way of life.

ANTHROPOLOGISTS studying the Paleolithic are particularly concerned with understanding how, over hundreds of thousands of years, the human body adapted to a changing environment. They are called physical anthropologists.

stone helps to
keep rotating
stick steady

△ These amazing carved clay bison, found in caves in France, are at least 12,000 years old.

THERE IS PLENTY OF EVIDENCE about what early people made and what they ate. Stone tools, pottery, carvings, paintings and even food refuse have been found on sites all over the world. The way people built their houses and treated their dead provides clues about how they organized their societies. But trying to understand their beliefs about life, death and the supernatural is much harder (see page 50).

THE MAKE IT WORK! way of looking at history is to ask questions of the past and find answers by making replicas of the things people made. But you do not have to make everything in the book to understand Stone Age people's way of life.

△ A Stone Age man uses a bow-drill to make a fire.

Timeline

The Stone Age covers the most remote part of human history. By studying Stone Age people, we can try to understand the **biological** development of human beings across the world. We can learn how people developed as social and spiritual beings, and how they survived and spread out, in spite of very harsh conditions.

LOOKING SO FAR BACK to investigate our early ancestors makes us realize how different their lives were. But it also shows us the characteristics that separate humans from all other animals.

HUMAN BEINGS DEVELOPED—in their physical build, the social groups they lived in, and the tools and weapons they used—at a gradually increasing speed. As a result, there is more to record over the last 10,000 years of the Stone Age than over the first three million years.

LOWER/MIDDLE PALEOLITHIC	3 million B.C.		2 million B.C.		1.5 million B.C.

Australopithecus *in existence*

Homo habilis *appear*

First hand axes

Homo erectus *appear*

MIDDLE/UPPER PALEOLITHIC	100,000 B.C.		50,000 B.C.		40,000 B.C.

Last ice age begins

Homo sapiens *appear in Africa*

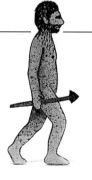

Homo sapiens *arrive in Australia*

First sea voyage

Mammoth-bone huts

MESOLITHIC/ NEOLITHIC	10,000 B.C.		8000 B.C.		6000 B.C.

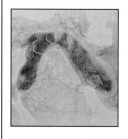

Making of pots in Near East

Farming and growth of permanent settlements in Near East (Fertile Crescent)

Earliest defended settlements, such as Jericho

Farming in Europe and China

THE ANCESTORS OF MODERN HUMANS first split off from the African apes between five and eight million years ago. But it took another several million years for *Homo sapiens,* or modern humans, to make an appearance (see page 12).

By that time, they were living in socially organized groups, had mastered hunting and gathering skills, discovered how to make fire, and equipped themselves with a basic, but effective, tool kit made of stones and pebbles.

THE CHART BELOW covers the entire Stone Age period we are looking at. However, the three bands relate to varying lengths of time: the top band spans three million years, while the bottom band covers just seven thousand years.

IN THIS BOOK we usually refer to the number of years B.C. (before the birth of Christ, nearly 2,000 years ago) to date an object or an event. There are times however, when we simply state how many years ago something happened.

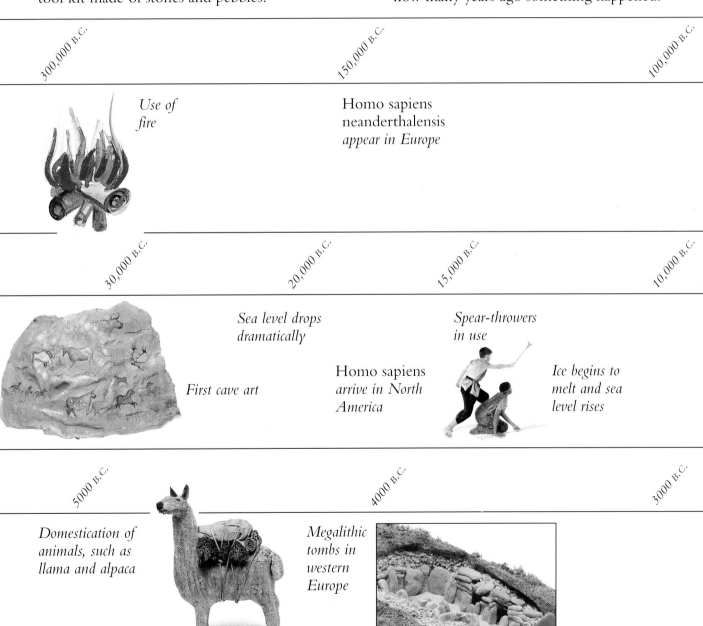

300,000 B.C.   150,000 B.C.   100,000 B.C.

Use of fire

Homo sapiens neanderthalensis *appear in Europe*

30,000 B.C.   20,000 B.C.   15,000 B.C.   10,000 B.C.

Sea level drops dramatically

First cave art

Homo sapiens *arrive in North America*

Spear-throwers in use

Ice begins to melt and sea level rises

5000 B.C.   4000 B.C.   3000 B.C.

Domestication of animals, such as llama and alpaca

Megalithic tombs in western Europe

A frozen world

About 1½ million years ago, the Earth started suffering periods of bitterly cold conditions known as "glacials" or ice ages. *Homo sapiens* appeared roughly when the last ice age began, 100,000 years ago. This ice age is known as the Würm in Europe, or the Wisconsin glacial in the United States.

AS THE TEMPERATURE DROPPED during the last ice age, ice sheets spread out to cover much of northern Europe and the mountains of North America. The ice was hundreds of yards thick. Freezing temperatures and strong, icy winds made many areas uninhabitable.

THE SEA LEVEL lowered because so much water was locked up in the ice sheets. At the coldest point, around 20,000 B.C., the sea was about 103 yards (100 meters) lower than it is today. As a result, land bridges joined Britain to Europe, North America to Asia, and Australia to New Guinea.

▽ *These are some of the animals that lived during the last ice age as shown on the map.*

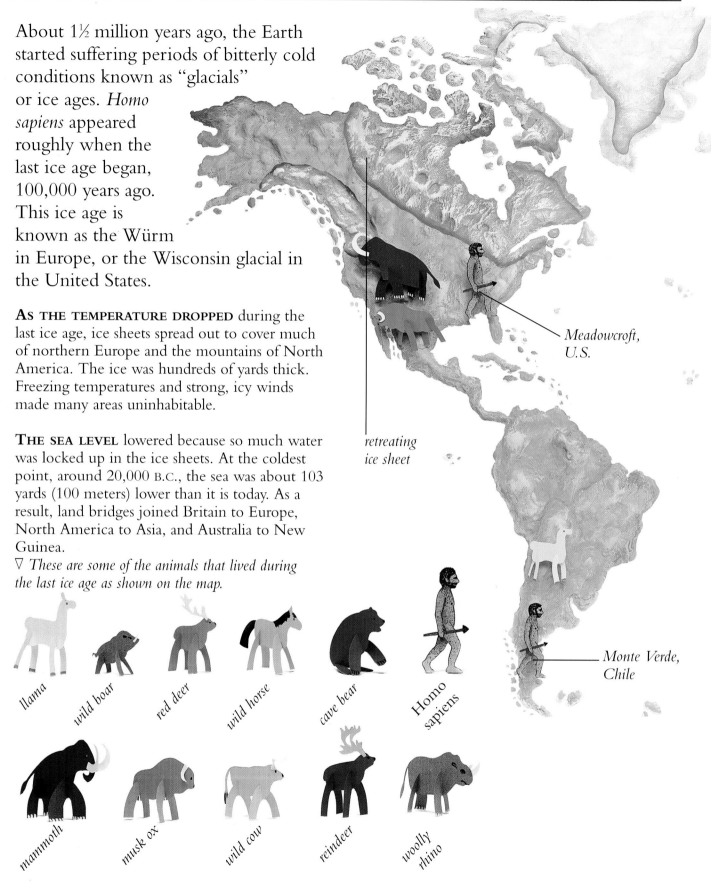

Meadowcroft, U.S.

retreating ice sheet

Monte Verde, Chile

llama

wild boar

red deer

wild horse

cave bear

Homo sapiens

mammoth

musk ox

wild cow

reindeer

woolly rhino

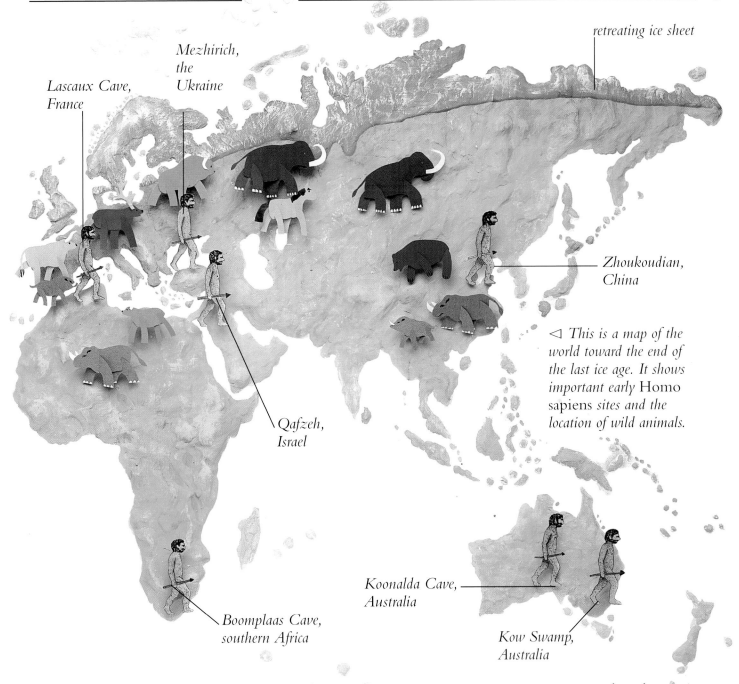

retreating ice sheet

Mezhirich, the Ukraine

Lascaux Cave, France

Zhoukoudian, China

◁ This is a map of the world toward the end of the last ice age. It shows important early Homo sapiens sites and the location of wild animals.

Qafzeh, Israel

Boomplaas Cave, southern Africa

Koonalda Cave, Australia

Kow Swamp, Australia

THE ICE BEGAN TO MELT and retreat and the sea level started to rise again around 15,000 years ago. The water slowly covered the existing land bridges, turning Britain into an island, and separating America from Asia, and Australia from New Guinea.

LARGE ANIMALS that had adapted to the cold, such as the mammoth and woolly rhinoceros, followed the retreating ice sheets north. When the ice retreated farther, they became **extinct**.

THE BARE, BLEAK LANDSCAPE at the edge of the ice sheets, which was covered in herbs and lichens and had very few trees, also moved northward. With it went the reindeer who lived on these plants.

GRADUALLY, THE CLIMATE became warmer and wetter. This brought more grasslands, forests, and edible plants, which suited the needs of smaller, faster animals such as deer and wild boar, and various birds and fish.

Back to our roots

No one is sure how or where *Homo sapiens* came into existence. We do know that humans and African apes once shared an ancestor and that the first **hominids**, or human ancestors, separated from the apes between five million and eight million years ago.

STONE AGE PEOPLE date back to the time when these hominids with human characteristics, such as bigger brains, different jaws, and **bipedalism**, or walking upright, emerged. By 100,000 years ago, while still living in the Stone Age, they had developed into what we call "modern humans."

△ *This is the skull of an* Australopithecus, *found by famous anthropologist Richard Leakey at Lake Turkana in Kenya. Its jawbone is missing.*

▽ *This is how Stone Age people developed.*

Australopithecus,
4 million years old

Homo habilis,
2 million years old

🐘 *AUSTRALOPITHECUS* were the first human ancestors. The oldest discovered fossils are around four million years old. They show that while this species had ape-sized brains, they walked upright. The most famous *Australopithecus* fossil is Lucy —surviving parts of her three-million-year-old skeleton were found in Ethiopia. The structure of her leg bones suggests that she was bipedal.

🐘 *HOMO IS THE SCIENTIFIC NAME* used for humans. The oldest discovered fossils referred to as *Homo* date back about two million years. The skeletons of ***Homo habilis*** resemble the *Australopithecus*, but they have larger brains, smaller jaws, and are more lightly built. Also, *Homo habilis*, which means "handy man," first developed the use of stone tools.

△ *Many cartoons printed in journals in the late 1800's made fun of Darwin's theory that humans descended from the apes.*

ONE OF THE FIRST PEOPLE to suggest that human beings descended from the apes was a man called Charles Darwin. Until the 1800's, it was generally accepted that God created human beings. But in 1859, Darwin caused an uproar in society when he published his theory of **natural evolution**.

In it, he claimed that groups of animals and plants changed as they struggled to exist. Nature selected the species that succeeded in surviving, with the result that some died out completely while new species emerged. Human beings he said, evolved, or changed, in the same way and because of this our ancestors could be traced back to prehistoric times.

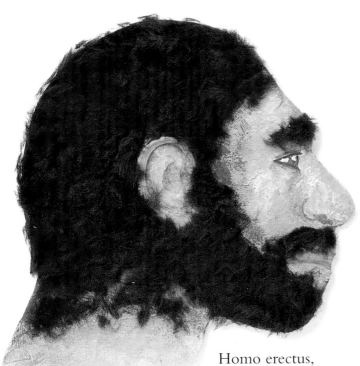

Homo erectus,
1.5 million years old

Homo sapiens,
100,000 years old

🐘 **HOMO ERECTUS,** which means "upright man," appeared around 1.5 million years ago. *Homo erectus* had a bigger brain and body and smaller teeth than *Homo habilis*. Like modern humans they used fire. They were also the first early human form found in places outside Africa. By 700,000 years ago, they had spread to southeast Asia and later to northern Asia and Europe.

🐘 **MODERN HUMANS** belong to a species known as *Homo sapiens*. They had much larger brains and were more lightly built and less muscular than earlier species. Perhaps these factors helped them adapt to the Earth's changing climate and conditions more easily. *Homo sapiens* were the first species to inhabit all the continents in the world.

🦣 **THERE ARE DIFFERENT THEORIES** about how and where modern humans emerged. Some experts believe they appeared first in southern Africa, perhaps as far back as 150,000 years ago, and then migrated to Europe, Asia, America, and Australia.

Others believe it is more likely that *Homo sapiens* eventually developed separately in different parts of Asia from *Homo erectus*, who had spread to the Far East almost a million years earlier. From Asia and Africa, the species then spread to the other continents of the world. So far, the earliest modern humans outside Africa have been found on two sites in Israel and date back to around 90,000 years ago.

△ *This trail of footprints is 3.6 million years old. It proves that hominids were upright walkers by this time.*

HOW HUMAN BEINGS EVOLVED

▽ *This chart shows important landmarks in the development of modern humans and their ancestors.*

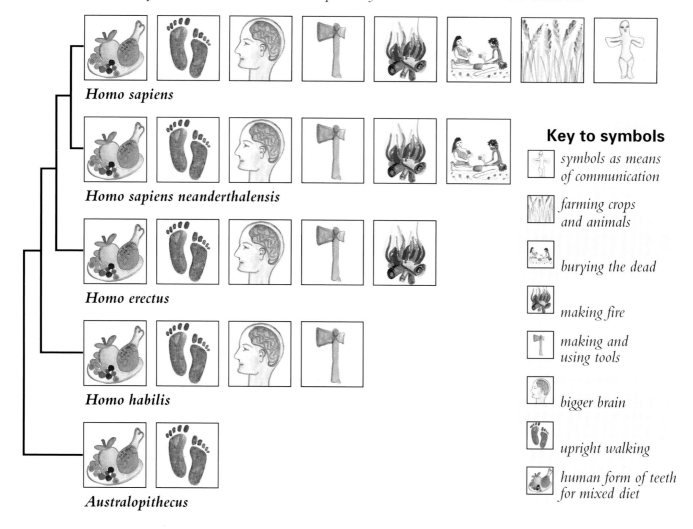

Homo sapiens

Homo sapiens neanderthalensis

Homo erectus

Homo habilis

Australopithecus

Key to symbols

- symbols as means of communication
- farming crops and animals
- burying the dead
- making fire
- making and using tools
- bigger brain
- upright walking
- human form of teeth for mixed diet

🐘 IN CHINA, *Homo sapiens* had appeared by 70,000 years ago and in Australia by around 50,000 years ago. Although land bridges existed between New Guinea and Australia at that time, there was still almost 62 miles (100 kilometers) of sea between Indonesia and New Guinea. So the arrival of *Homo sapiens* in Australia shows that they managed to make some sort of seagoing craft for the journey (see page 44).

🐘 🏃 THE NEANDERTHALS *(Homo sapiens neanderthalensis)* first appeared in Europe about 150,000 years ago, though no one is sure exactly where they came from. Remains show that both sexes were stocky in build with a long, low skull, heavy jaw, and receding chin. Neanderthals became extinct about 35,000 years ago.

🏃 A NEW TYPE OF EARLY human had arrived in central and western Europe by 40,000 years ago. They are called **Cro-Magnon** after the French cave where some of the earliest remains of modern humans were found. The Cro-Magnons were tall, long-limbed, and similar in build to people who live in warm climates today.

Finally, around 15,000 years ago when the sea level was at its lowest, the first group of *Homo sapiens* walked across the land bridge in the Bering Straits from Asia to North America.

🐘 TOOL-MAKING was crucial to the development of the human species. Hand axes, which were first made around 1.5 million years ago were very successful tools.

WARNING! DO NOT MAKE OR USE A HAND AX WITHOUT THE HELP OF AN ADULT.

▷ *A 700,000-year-old hand ax. It was probably used by* Homo erectus.

People continued to use these tools for over a million years. They were elongated and symmetrical with a sharp cutting edge. Today they are the earliest solid evidence experts have to help them understand the survival techniques of early hominids.

HOW A HAND AX CAN BE MADE

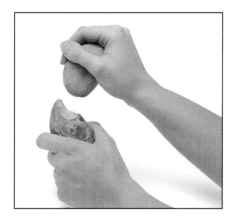

1 *The first flake is chipped from the side of a stone to create a point.*

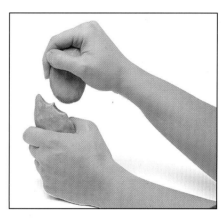

2 *A sharp edge emerges with the second blow to the same side.*

3 *The third blow lengthens the existing sharp, cutting edge.*

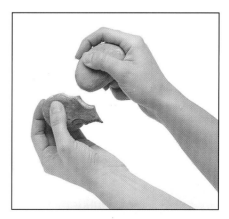

4 *Flakes are struck from the other side to sharpen the point.*

Safety in numbers

From the beginning, *Homo sapiens* seems to have understood that it was better to live and hunt with a larger group of people than just a single family. There was safety in numbers from dangerous wild animals and maybe even from other bands of hunters chasing the same prey. Hunting in groups could also make it easier to trap and kill powerful creatures such as bison and mammoth.

✻ DIFFERENT PLANTS AND ANIMALS were available as the seasons changed. This meant that many early hunters lived away from their base camp sometimes. In Denmark for example, some **hunter–gatherers** moved to different places at certain times of the year, setting up temporary camps along the way.

During the winter, they camped inland, deep in the forest near a stream or a lake. Some hunters went in search of wild boar, elks, and **aurochs**— wild cows—for their meat. Smaller animals, such as beavers and foxes, were hunted for their warm pelts.

WHEN SPRING CAME, hunting continued inland as the groups relied mainly on red deer for their food supply. This was also the season when some members returned to the coast to hunt seals.

As the weather warmed up, the groups moved nearer to the sea and built a camp of branch huts near an inland stream or lake. This way they could travel easily to the coast to fish for cod and mackerel.

THE HUNTERS USED WEAPONS, such as bows and arrows, spears and clubs, which were made of bone or wood. Harpoons for fishing were often carved from deer antlers. People gathered fruits, plants, and nuts throughout the year. Supplies of these were stored for times when meat and fish were scarce.

women gathering fruits and nuts

fishing from hollow tree-trunk boats

seals

MAKE A HARPOON AND THROWING STICK

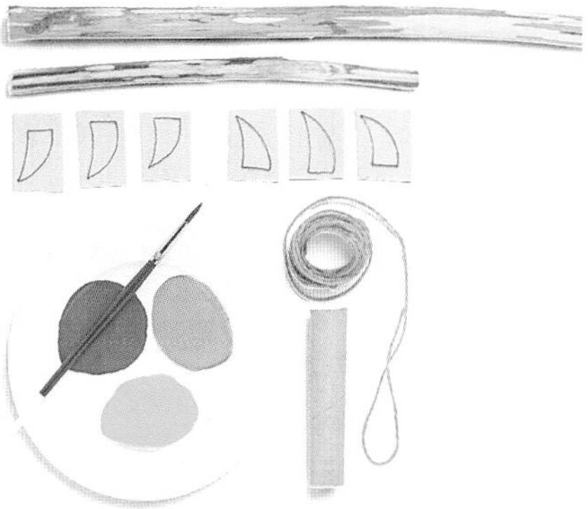

You will need: two sticks: one, 17 in. (50 cm), one 7 in. (22 cm); thin cardboard, cardboard tube 4 in. (10 cm), paints, twine, glue, craft knife

1 Glue the tube on the longer stick, leaving half hanging over the end. Draw six blades on the cardboard and cut them out.

2 Ask an adult to help you cut three slits, evenly spaced, down each side of the shorter stick. Glue a blade into each slit.

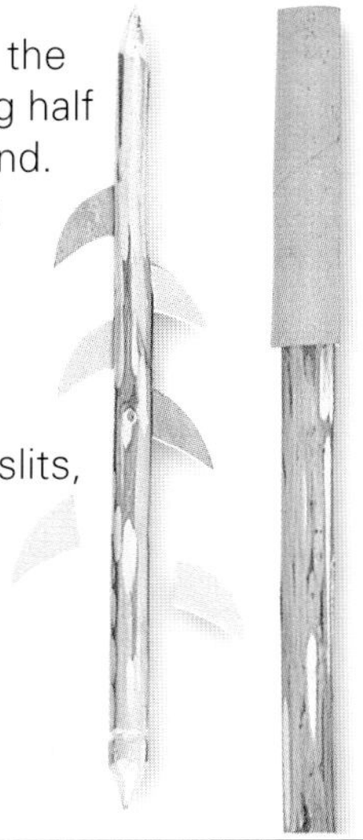

3 Now ask an adult to help you sharpen each end of the harpoon into a point.

4 Wrap twine around the end of the tube. Wrap more twine farther up where the tube extends over the stick, leaving enough twine to wind around and attach the harpoon as shown at right. Paint the harpoon and the shaft brownish-grey.

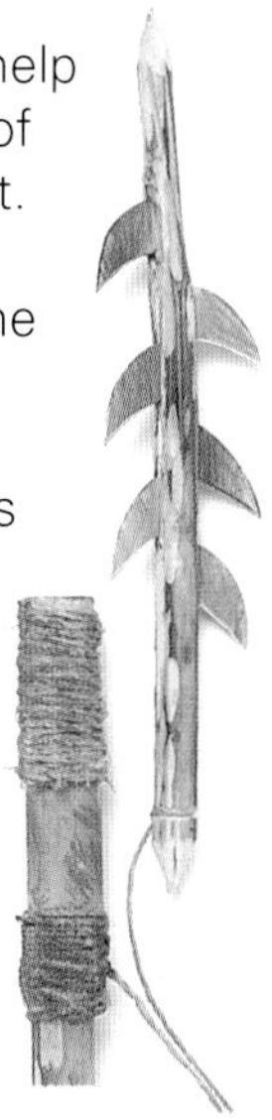

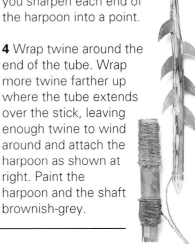

WARNING! NEVER THROW THIS HARPOON AT A LIVING THING.

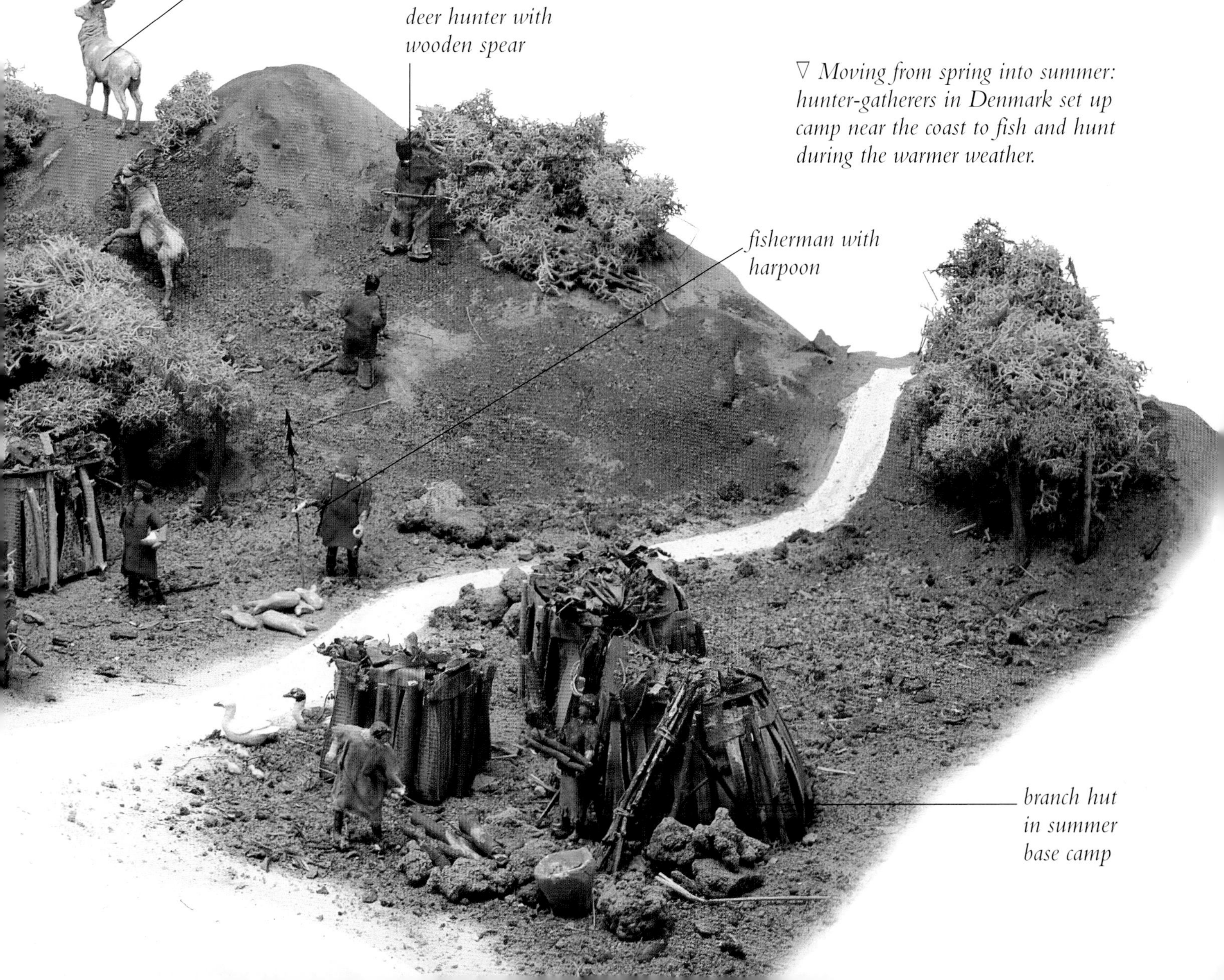
red deer
deer hunter with wooden spear
fisherman with harpoon
branch hut in summer base camp

▽ *Moving from spring into summer: hunter-gatherers in Denmark set up camp near the coast to fish and hunt during the warmer weather.*

Shelter from the elements

Even the earliest **nomadic** humans needed shelters to survive. At first, these were basic dwellings such as caves and huts made of branches and leaves. As people began to lead more settled lives, they wanted more permanent homes. The place where they lived, the climate and the raw materials and tools available, determined the types of houses they built.

EARLY HUMANS sheltered in caves they found as they wandered in search of food. Caves protected them from the rain and kept them warm in winter and cool in summer. Fossilized remains of some of the earliest hominids have been found in the limestone caves of southern Africa.

EVIDENCE OF some of the oldest man-made shelters has been discovered in areas of southern Africa where caves are rare. Here, early people stuck small branches into the ground and supported them by piling stones around their base. Bringing the branches together at the top and perhaps weaving grass among the leaves and twigs provided them with shade from the blazing African sun.

ABOUT 13,000 YEARS AGO, a group of hunter-gatherers made a riverside settlement at Monte Verde in southern Chile. The walls of the 12 rectangular dwellings were made of a wooden framework covered by the hides of **mastodons** (extinct elephants). Inside each hut, a shallow, clay-lined pit held coals for warmth. Cooking probably took place outside at large communal hearths.

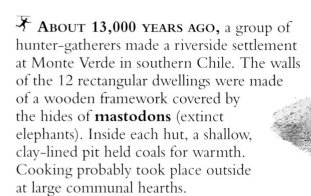

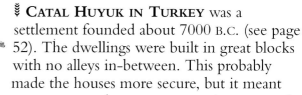

❧ **CATAL HUYUK IN TURKEY** was a settlement founded about 7000 B.C. (see page 52). The dwellings were built in great blocks with no alleys in-between. This probably made the houses more secure, but it meant there was no way in at ground level. Therefore people had to walk across the rooftops and climb in by ladder. The thatched roofs were supported by wooden beams that rested on the mud-brick walls. Inside, each house had fitted benches and platforms, a hearth, and a built-in clay oven.

❧ **NEAR THE RIVER DANUBE** in Serbia are the remains of Lepenski Vir, a settlement of tent-like **trapezoidal** houses dating from about 6000 B.C. Up to 100 people may have lived there. The walls of the houses were made of wooden poles fixed to a central ridge and then covered with reed thatch. Inside, beyond a stone threshold, the floor was plastered with limestone. A hearth stood near the door.

❧ **AROUND 6000 B.C., BANPO,** a settlement in northern China, was built (see page 39). The dwellings were either pyramid-shaped or circular and about four steps below ground level. People entered them by a long, low porch. Thatched roofs were supported on four large posts set in a square. Most of the houses had clay-plastered floors and a sunken fire pit set into the center.

🏃 **A SHORTAGE OF RAW MATERIALS** never stopped early *Homo sapiens* from building shelters. Some of the most amazing homes lived in by Stone Age hunters are the mammoth–bone huts of southern Russia and the Ukraine. These were built between 15,000 and 40,000 years ago.

UP TO SIX HUNDRED MAMMOTH BONES, including skulls, jawbones, tusks, leg, and toe bones, went into the construction of each hut. It is thought that the largest hut used bones from more than a hundred different mammoths.

These bones would have come from both mammoths that died naturally and those that were hunted. Primarily, mammoths were killed for the mountains of meat they provided. It was so cold that people could store surplus meat in holes dug in the ground. There was enough flesh on one mammoth to feed a family for a whole year.

JAWBONES, SKULLS, AND LEG BONES were used to build a base for the huts. They were also used to support the tusks and wooden poles which formed a roof that was probably arched.

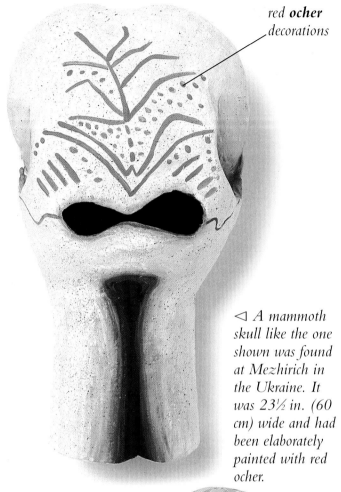

*red **ocher** decorations*

◁ *A mammoth skull like the one shown was found at Mezhirich in the Ukraine. It was 23½ in. (60 cm) wide and had been elaborately painted with red ocher.*

🦣 **MAKE A MAMMOTH-BONE HUT**

You will need: 3⅓ yd. (3 m) brown fur fabric, thick cardboard, twigs, double-sided adhesive tape, paints, string, large pebbles

1 Cut four cardboard strips, 3 yd. x 2 in. (2.6 m x 5 cm) and seven strips, 20½ x 2 in. (52 x 5 cm). Cut several thinner strips, 20½ x 1 in. (52 x 3 cm). Cut out the bone and tusk shapes as shown at left. Paint these off-white. Cut the fabric into big, rough shapes.

2 Lay one of the large cardboard strips flat on the floor. Place the other three large strips over it, spacing them out to make a star. Tape to secure. Ask a friend to hold this up to create a dome. Tape the seven shorter 2-in. (5-cm)-wide strips around the base.

THE GAPS BETWEEN THE BONES may have been packed with grass and moss. Animal hides were probably stretched over the framework and held down with mammoth jaws to stop them from tearing in the wild winds. Turf may also have been used on the outer layer.

△ *Mammoths looked like hairy elephants with huge curved tusks. They lived in cold parts of the world.*

ARCHAEOLOGISTS BELIEVE it may have taken four people a week to build one of these huts. And it must have been hard work: some of the tusks weighed up to 440 pounds (200 kilograms).

3 Now, working upward, tape the thinner strips horizontally around the dome to reinforce its shape and make it stronger. You will probably need three or four such rows of struts. Make sure there is an equal distance between each row.

4 Tie a small bundle of twigs with string. Attach it to the top of the hut with tape. Next, tape the pieces of fabric to the hut frame. Work from the bottom upward to make sure the fur overlaps and there are no gaps.

5 Using string, tie one pair of tusks together at the tip so that they cross over each other. Tape them above the hut entrance. Add another tusk on each side. Lean the bones around the base of the hut. Finally, use the pebbles to build a hearth inside.

MAMMOTH-BONE HUTS may have been kept warm inside by lining them with hides. At the mammoth-bone hut site in Mezhirich in the Ukraine, evidence of hearths containing ash and charcoal were found. As well as being used for cooking, these hearths helped to heat the dwellings.

The inside area of the huts was about 23 to 26 yards (7 to 8 meters) in diameter. This was large enough for four or five people to live fairly comfortably, but still small enough to keep reasonably warm.

FLINT TOOLS, BONE NEEDLES, and **awls,** and simple ornaments of bone and amber, have all been found on the sites. They indicate that these huts really were homes where people lived.

AS PEOPLE SETTLED in one place more permanently, and particularly as they learned to farm crops and breed animals, they began to live in larger communities of hamlets and villages (see page 30). Some of these may have been no bigger than hunter bands, while others were villages with populations of several hundred.

IN THE UKRAINE, villages of 20 to 40 long-houses were emerging by 4000 B.C. Each one was 66 to 131 feet (20 to 40 meters) long and probably housed extended families of perhaps 10 to 15 people.

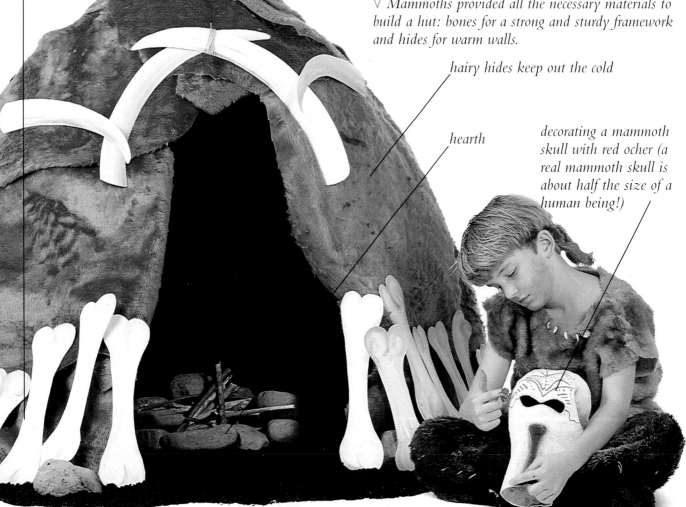

bones hold down hides to prevent tearing in the wind

▽ *Mammoths provided all the necessary materials to build a hut: bones for a strong and sturdy framework and hides for warm walls.*

hairy hides keep out the cold

hearth

decorating a mammoth skull with red ocher (a real mammoth skull is about half the size of a human being!)

In some cases, the houses were arranged in a rough circle with one or two buildings in the center—perhaps the home of a chieftain, or even a communal hall. Similar longhouses are found in villages in eastern and central Europe.

▷ *Mammoth-bone huts and later, longhouses, kept out the severe cold of the icy Russian climate.*

IN NORTHERN CHINA during the same period, villages were made up of individual round and square dwellings, each large enough to house only a single family. Here, too, there were sometimes larger buildings which may have been a ceremonial center for the entire village.

MAKE A LONGHOUSE

1 Paint a brown criss-cross pattern onto two 7 x 2 in. roof sections. Glue twigs to the two smallest side sections of house and to one end section. Mix plaster with gravel and water and apply to larger side sections and the other end section.

2 Paint the base brown. Mark house outline, 7 x 3½ in. (18 x 9 cm), and using the skewer, make holes about every ¾ in. (2 cm) around it. Cut skewers to match height of side and end sections. Glue in holes. Cut more for rafters and glue in position.

3 Glue twig and plaster-covered sides to framework as shown. One of the plastered sections is shorter to leave space for a doorway. Glue on roof sections. Glue hay on top.

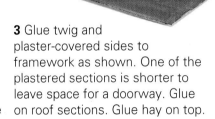

You will need: twigs cut to 1½ in. (4 cm), wooden skewers, paints, hay, plaster powder, gravel, glue, cardboard pieces: two 7 x 2 in. (18 x 6 cm), two 1¾ x 1½ in. (5 x 4 cm), one 5 x 1½ in. (13 x 4 cm), one 4¼ x 1½ in. (1 x 4 cm); two end sections: 3½ in. (9 cm) wide x 2¾ in. (7 cm) at point; base: 10 x 5½ in. (25 x 14 cm).

4 Smear glue on base surround and sprinkle gravel or soil on top to give the longhouse a rural setting.

IN 1850, THE REMAINS OF SKARA BRAE, a 5,000-year-old settlement on the west coast of the island of Orkney off northern Scotland, were exposed by a violent sea storm. This semi-subterranean village consists of seven houses linked together by narrow alleys. These were surrounded by a mound of **midden**, made up of rotten vegetables, dung, bones, stones, and shells. This must have smelled awful, but it protected the houses from rough weather.

▷ *One of the houses of Skara Brae.*

thick walls built from stone slabs collected from the beach

watertight stone box for shellfish

box bed with bracken mattress and skin canopy

dresser used for storage and display

THE ROOFS were probably made of turf, perhaps over a layer of animal skins, and were supported on whalebone rafters. In the center, a hole must have been left open to allow smoke to escape from the family hearth.

INDIVIDUAL HOUSES were roughly square and consisted of one main room with alcoves set into the walls. These may have been for storage, though some have drains running underneath so they could have been used as toilets. Doorways, only 3 feet (1 meter) high and 1½ feet (0.5 meter) wide, were closed by a stone slab held in place with a wooden or whalebone bar. Their small size was probably the best way to keep Orkney's freezing winds at bay.

△ *Today, a narrow stretch of sand separates Skara Brae from the sea. But when people lived there, sand dunes lay between the village and the water.*

FURNITURE from the Stone Age is rare, but it survives at Skara Brae because it was built of stone. The large boxes against the wall are thought to be beds. People may have used bracken and heather to make mattresses and animal-skin blankets to keep warm.

WALL CUPBOARDS or recesses above the beds may have held personal trinkets. A dresser, with stone slab shelves and legs, was found facing the door in every house. It was most likely the main place to store things such as cooking pots, large containers, and animal hides.

THE HEARTH in the middle of the main room would have been used for cooking as well as for heating the house. Wood was probably too precious to burn, so fuel would have been a mixture of animal dung, dried seaweed and grasses, and even whalebone.

THE BOXES by the hearth have been sealed with clay to make them watertight. As the people of Skara Brae probably fished a lot, the boxes could have been used for soaking limpets for fishbait.

From fur to fabric

Stone Age people wore clothing mainly to provide protection from the elements, especially the bitter cold. Skins and furs were best for this, but they also acted as a means of camouflage for hunters and warriors. Later, as clothing became more sophisticated, it could show a person's rank in society. Clay figurines, cave paintings, and remains found in well-preserved burial sites give us some idea of what Stone Age people wore.

SKINS AND FURS were worn by early people because they were warm and available. First, flint scrapers were used to clean the fat, grease, and dried blood off the inside of the skins. They were then washed and stretched as they dried. By rubbing with smooth stones and bones, the skins could be kept soft and supple.

TAILORING GARMENTS from skins required flint knives to cut them up, and flint or bone awls to punch holes for sewing the pieces together. Bone needles and twine made from sinews or vegetable fiber were used to stitch the skins together.

MAKE A STONE AGE OUTFIT

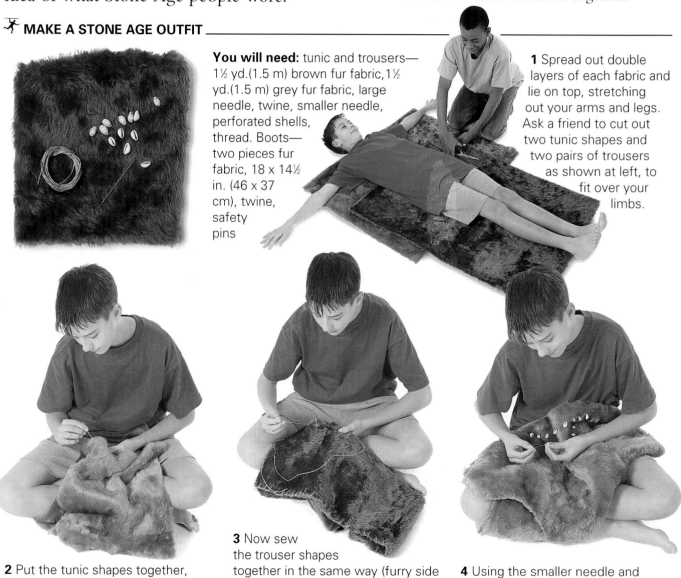

You will need: tunic and trousers— 1½ yd.(1.5 m) brown fur fabric, 1½ yd.(1.5 m) grey fur fabric, large needle, twine, smaller needle, perforated shells, thread. Boots— two pieces fur fabric, 18 x 14½ in. (46 x 37 cm), twine, safety pins

1 Spread out double layers of each fabric and lie on top, stretching out your arms and legs. Ask a friend to cut out two tunic shapes and two pairs of trousers as shown at left, to fit over your limbs.

2 Put the tunic shapes together, with the furry side facing out. Thread the large needle with twine and sew the two together.

3 Now sew the trouser shapes together in the same way (furry side out). Your stitches can be large and uneven as this is how Stone Age people would have sewn them.

4 Using the smaller needle and thread, sew some shells onto the front of tunic and, if you like, down outside edges of the trouser legs.

◁ *This Stone Age man adds the finishing touches to his warm, furry outfit with a bearskin headband.*

△ *A Victorian engraving showing a bearskin being stretched and scraped clean.*

✦ **THE REMAINS** of an old man buried in Russia about 20,000 B.C. give us some clues about clothing worn at that time. His hat had 24 fox teeth sewed on it, and lots of ivory beads, which probably decorated his clothes, lay in rows across his body. His outfit would have possibly included a shirt, long trousers, fur boots, and a fur cloak.

fur tunics would have been made of bearskin or deerskin

MAKE THE BOOTS

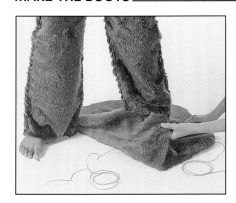

1 Place one piece of fur on the floor (furry side down). Slip 3½ ft.(1.2 m) twine under it near the front, leaving even lengths on both sides. Put your foot on the fur toward the front.

2 Ask a friend to help you fold the fur securely over your foot, starting at the front. Pin to hold in place. Continue to fold and tuck the fur up your leg until you reach the top.

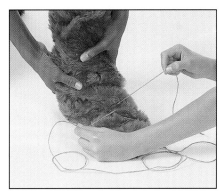

3 Cross twine over your foot and ankle and criss-cross all the way to the top of fur, pulling in tightly (but so that the boot feels comfortable). Tie and cut off surplus twine.

MAKING FABRIC WAS A BIG STEP forward in producing clothes. It offered lots of new and different textures and the opportunity to dye cloth in various colors and to make patterns within the material. Along with jewelry, it meant that Stone Age people could decorate themselves and think more about their appearance.

⚘ **THE EARLIEST FIBERS** used by humans to make clothing may have been the plant fibers made into cord about 10,000 B.C. in Peru and the state of Utah. By stitching long lengths of cord to a belt, it could be used to make a skirt.

▷ *A Neolithic woman spinning wool. She is wearing a linen dress and a decorated purse. It is believed that people sometimes used clay stamps to apply patterns like the one on this purse to cloth.*

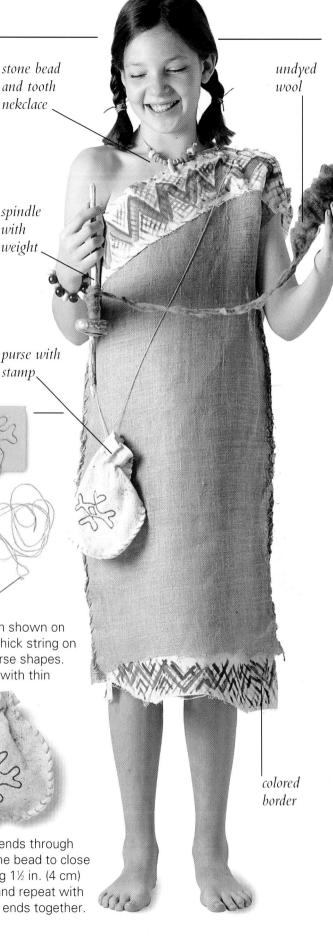

stone bead and tooth nekclace

undyed wool

spindle with weight

purse with stamp

colored border

⚘ **MAKE A PATTERNED PURSE**

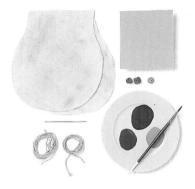

You will need: two pieces of cotton cloth cut in purse shape as shown, stiff cardboard, 4¾ in.(12 cm) square, beads, thick and thin string, paints, glue, darning needle

1 Draw stamp pattern shown on the cardboard. Glue thick string on top. Flick paint on purse shapes. Sew edges together with thin string.

2 Paint stamp pattern red and print it on the purse. Thread thin string through the top with long stitches, leaving long lengths at either end.

3 Thread both string ends through one bead and push the bead to close purse. Knot one string 1½ in. (4 cm) from end, add bead and repeat with other string. Tie both ends together.

⚜ **IN TURKEY BY 6000 B.C.,** wool was being spun on simple spindles with weights (or whorls), and flax was being harvested to make linen. Farther east in China, a plant fiber called **hemp** was being used to make cloth by 2000 B.C.

⚜ **DYEING AND WEAVING** were probably invented as early as spinning. On simple looms that lay flat rather than standing upright, wool was woven into cloth. Flowers, leaves, and tree bark were used to dye materials in reds, yellows, and browns. Minerals produced greens and blues. Figurines showing women in dresses and skirts with zigzag and checkered patterns suggest that the Stone Age weavers soon learned how to make good use of their colored wools.

🐘🏃⚜ **JEWELRY,** worn by men, women and children, consisted mainly of necklaces. People made these by stringing perforated seashells, animal teeth, or beads of soft stone, such as amber, on cord or twine. Sometimes, pendants were hung from the center of a necklace.

SOME SEASHELLS were so valued they were traded over great distances. The teeth of wolves and bears may have been worn to demonstrate the skill and bravery of hunters.

△ *This jewelry from India was made around 7000 B.C. from bone, shell, and limestone beads.*

🐘🏃⚜ **BODY PAINTING** was probably common but there is little evidence to prove it. The "paint" would have been made by grinding up ocher and black pigments mixed with animal fat, and then adding water. A lump of red ocher found with some sharp needles in a cave in the Pyrenees suggests that tattooing may have been practiced since 9000 B.C.

🏃 **MAKE A NECKLACE**

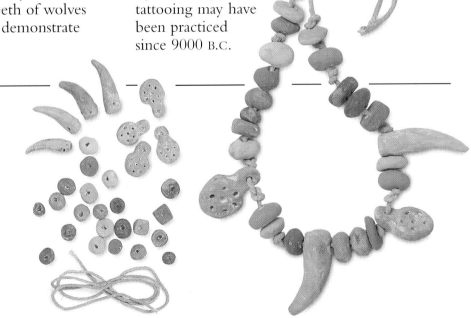

You will need: self-hardening clay, string, paints (natural colors), thick needle

1 Roll the clay into rough bead and tooth shapes as shown. Make holes in the beads with a needle. Leave to dry. Paint the beads, rubbing the wet paint to give a washed-out look.

2 Paint the string yellow. Thread beads, knotting at irregular intervals. Make a knot before the first bead and another after the last. Leave enough string at both ends to tie.

Hunting, fishing and farming

Prehistoric garbage dumps are important sources of information about what Stone Age people ate. Butchered bones tell us which animals were used for meat. Seeds, shells, and charred cereal grains reveal what plants and fruits were gathered or grown. Human skeletons may show wear and decay in teeth revealing the food that was eaten.

🐘 **OUR MOST ANCIENT ANCESTORS** were partly scavengers and partly hunters. In the beginning, they probably obtained most of the meat in their diet by scavenging the remains of animals that had been killed by other carnivores. They may have used their stone axes to cut up carcasses more than to make a kill.

△ *These Neolithic stone spearheads and arrowheads were found in different parts of Britain.*

🏃 MAKE A SPEAR AND SPEAR-THROWER

 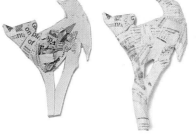 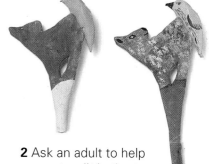

You will need: newspaper, flour and water paste, string, glue, three cotton circles, cardboard, three pieces of bamboo 26 in. (67 cm) long, wood 19½ in. (50 cm) long, paint, paper, craft knife, leather thong

1 Cut out the deer and bird shapes from cardboard, and glue together. Build up with papier-mâché using tiny strips of newspaper. Use enough layers to make the bird's tail solid but still able to fit into the bamboo.

2 Ask an adult to help you cut a slit in the top of the wood using a craft knife. Insert the animal shape and glue. Smooth over the joined parts with papier-mâché. Paint. Tie thong to the other end.

 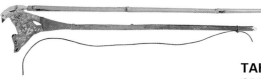

3 For the spears, glue a ball of newspaper on the end of each bamboo pole. Place a cotton circle on top and tie with string to secure.

4 Slot tail of the bird into hollow bamboo. To throw spear, wrap the leather thong around your wrist, hold spear-thrower above your shoulder and hurl spear at a target.

TAKE CARE—NEVER THROW SPEARS AT A LIVING THING.

To use: make a target of some wild animals you have painted, such as mammoths, woolly rhinos, and cave bears. Pin them to a tree or a tall fence, stand back and fire!

▽ *The remains of a fish trap like this, dating from 4000 B.C., were found in a bog site in Denmark.*

🏃 **WEAPONS AND WAYS OF CATCHING** animals were gradually developed by early humans. The first spears were made of wood with a tip hardened by charring in a fire. By 15,000 B.C., wooden and bone spear-throwers were being used to give hunters greater power and range. Often, these were carved with animal designs.

🌾 **BOWS AND ARROWS** came increasingly into use after the ice age. Bows of yew and elm, about 6½ feet (2 meters) long, and feather-flighted pine arrows dating from 8000 B.C. have been found in northern Europe.

Spears and bows and arrows were used for fishing too, but new methods were developed after the ice age. In Denmark around 5000 B.C., basketwork traps were laid in rivers and bone hooks on lines were used. In Scandinavia and Japan, nets made of twine were weighted with stone rings to catch ocean fish.

spear-thrower attached to wrist

SHELLFISH were another source of seafood, and dumps or middens of shells are found around coastal zones all over the world. Shell middens are often huge. Some discovered in Europe measure 109 by 44 yards (100 by 40 meters) and are up to 10 feet (3 meters) deep.

hunter launches spear using spear-thrower

🏃🌾 **A SEASONAL CYCLE** involved gathering shellfish as well as collecting summer fruits, nuts and edible plants. Communities in eastern Japan followed a cycle like this from 10,000 B.C. Middens indicate that over 30 species of shellfish were eaten. Plant food was an important part of the diet too. Over 180 types of plant have been identified from various Japanese settlements.

◁ *Spear-throwers enabled Stone Age hunters to kill bigger prey from farther away.*

❧ **THE CHANGE FROM HUNTING** to farming was a long process and happened at different times everywhere. It first occurred 10,000 years ago in the **Fertile Crescent** – an arc of land stretching from southern Iraq and Iran northward through Syria and down through Lebanon and Palestine. Farming emerged separately in Europe, North Africa, China, and New Guinea before 6000 B.C. and in South America in 5000 B.C.

▽ *A central European farming village in autumn.*

△ *Cereals grew wild in the Fertile Crescent, which may have encouraged farming to develop there first.*

fields being plowed for the next planting

garbage pit

longhouse where families live

WILD FORMS OF WHEAT AND BARLEY grew naturally around the Fertile Crescent, so people may have started planting these near their homes where they could be tended easily. Watering, weeding, and selecting the best grains to plant eventually led to bigger grains and more crops. Later, where conditions allowed, pulses and legumes, such as lentils and peas, were grown in the Fertile Crescent too.

THE FIRST CROPS TO BE FARMED varied from country to country. Millet and rice were grown in China, taro (a root crop) and bananas in New Guinea, maize (corn) in South America and squash, peppers, and avocados in Mexico.

FARMING HAD A MAJOR impact on people's lifestyles. It meant they had to settle in one place and tend their crops. They also had to look after their newly domesticated, or tamed, animals in order to breed or rear them for meat and milk.

In winter, food supplies had to be stored and protective shelters built. As a result, early farming was often accompanied by the growth of permanent settlements – either farms or villages.

But in areas where there was lots of wild food to support the population, the switch to farming was very gradual. Hunting and gathering was so successful in southern Africa for example, that the people continued to practice it there until a few hundred years ago.

wooden trackway

fishing net drying

animal skin drying

covered working area

river for water and fish supplies

sheep pen

LEARNING HOW TO MAKE FIRE was one of the human race's major discoveries. Early hominids probably found animals that had been cooked by bush fires and may even have used the embers of these fires for light and heat. But evidence of hearths in caves and open sites in Europe and Asia show that it wasn't until 300,000 years ago that fire-lighting was discovered.

BY GATHERING TINDER—dry grass and small pieces of dry wood and bark—and rubbing two sticks vigorously against each other in the center of the tinder, a fire can be started in minutes.

BY PERHAPS 4000 B.C., in both Eurasia and America, the process of making fire had become easier as people were using bow-drills. These were small bows about 12 inches (30 cm) long. The string was twisted around a stick standing upright in the tinder, which was rotated back and forth very fast. Fragments of these bow-drills have been found in the Guitarrero Cave in Peru.

COOKING WITHOUT USING POTS was common for Stone Age people. Meat was either roasted on a spit over a fire, or baked in the embers by wrapping it in large leaves.

▷ *Preparing a cooked meal in Neolithic Europe—the use of a bow-drill made fire-lighting easier and quicker.*

bow-drill being used to light fire

bark container

tinder made up of dry wood and bark

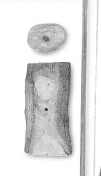

3 Hold the clay stone, dented side down, and fit it into top of dowel rod. Place pointed end of dowel rod in hole in wood. Twist it fast to make fire.

You will need: string, dowel rods, self-hardening clay, block of wood, willow twig, paints, craft knife

NEVER USE A BOW-DRILL WITHOUT AN ADULT. FIRES CAN CAUSE ACCIDENTS.

1 Mold the clay into an oval. Make a dent in the side. When dry, paint it to look like a stone. Ask an adult to help cut a small hole in the wood's center and to sharpen one end of the rod to fit into this.

2 Tie string to one end of the twig. Lay the twig across the middle of the rod. Wrap string around the rod and tie it to the other end of the twig, allowing it to bend slightly.

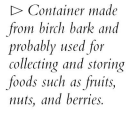

▷ *Container made from birch bark and probably used for collecting and storing foods such as fruits, nuts, and berries.*

clay pots used for storing fruit, vegetables, and grains

PRE-HEATED STONES, known as pot boilers, were also used. They could heat water in skin containers before food was boiled in them. Or they could be placed in shallow ground with food and then covered with earth.

CLAY POTS for cooking or storing food were another great step forward. People started making them soon after the beginnings of farming. Because clay pots do not catch fire, they could be put directly on a hearth or in an oven and food could be safely left to cook in them for long periods at an even temperature.

❧ **ONCE PEOPLE SET UP FARMS,** they could eat meat more regularly. Sheep and goats were the earliest domesticated animals reared for their meat, though they continued to live wild around the Fertile Crescent. The wild pig and wild forms of cattle were domesticated across Eurasia by 6000 B.C.

EVEN WITHOUT MEAT, the prehistoric diet was surprisingly varied. And with the use of fire, food could be prepared in different ways too. Vegetables and plants could be boiled together into stews, and fruit could be poached or preserved in jams and jellies.

◁ *Early digging sticks were weighted at one end and used to dig up edible plants.*

❧ **TRANSFORMING THE EARS** of edible grasses into flour to make bread is one of the many achievements of early farmers. The first fields were dug with hoes made from forked branches or digging sticks with one pointed end and a stone weight at the other. But by 3000 B.C., cattle-drawn plows— usually made of branches—were in use in Europe, the Near East, and China.

goat   *cow*

pig   *sheep*

△ *These wild creatures are believed to look very similar to the earliest domesticated animals.*

❧ **SICKLES FOR HARVESTING** wild grasses appeared in Egypt around 15,000 B.C. They had bone or wooden handles with short flint blades set in them. The same models remained in use for thousands of years in many parts of the world.

🐘 **MAKE A WILD FRUIT COMPOTE**

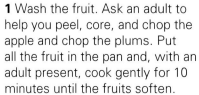

You will need: blackberries, red currants, sloes, plums, apple, honey, a small pan, a wooden spoon

1 Wash the fruit. Ask an adult to help you peel, core, and chop the apple and chop the plums. Put all the fruit in the pan and, with an adult present, cook gently for 10 minutes until the fruits soften.

2 Stir in 1 or 2 Tblesps. honey to sweeten and continue stewing for another few minutes. Serve your fruit compote warm or cold, by itself or with cream or yogurt.

◁ *This flint sickle was found in the River Thames in London. It could be as much as 6,000 years old.*

AFTER THE CORN was **threshed** and **winnowed**, the grains were ground down. Neolithic farmers everywhere used a quern, a large flat stone, and a smaller oval stone pestle for doing this. The daily grinding of grain into coarse flour by rubbing it backward and forward on the quern using the pestle, gradually wore down the center of the millstones. That is why they are sometimes referred to as saddle-querns.

Stone Age people probably used large shells as dishes where they were available

⚡ **BAKING OVENS WERE AN EARLY** invention of Neolithic farmers and they appear at Abu Hureyra in Syria around 9000 B.C. and Jarmo in Iraq around 6000 B.C. Made of mud or mud-brick, they are usually round or horseshoe-shaped and have a dome roof.

FLOUR WAS MIXED WITH WATER to make dough that was molded into loaves and baked in these ovens. The same dough was used to make smaller, flat drop scones. These were cooked on a stone hot plate over an open fire.

▷ *Enjoying a tasty compote: fruits probably varied according to the season.*

Ancient art

Some of the finest Stone Age art still survives today in cave and rock paintings and engravings in parts of Europe, Asia, Africa, and Australia. In Europe alone, over 200 caves with examples of this art have been found.

THE EARLIEST CAVE PAINTINGS are from France, possibly dating back to 30,000 B.C. Examples found in Saharan Africa were painted around 20,000 B.C., while the earliest Australian rock art may be even older.

Many cave paintings in Spain or France are found deep in caves where there is no natural light. The painters must have worked in the flickering light of brushwood torches, or lamps made by burning fur or moss soaked in animal fat. They applied their paint with either their fingers or "brushes" made of hair.

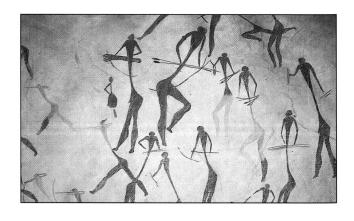

△ *Hunters armed with bows and arrows were painted on the rocks at Valltorta, Spain, around 6000 B.C.*

THE EARTHY COLORS they used—red, yellow, brown and black—came from minerals such as ocher, manganese, and charcoal. These were ground to powder and mixed with animal fat to make a sticky paint that adhered to cave walls and ceilings. The colors are still bright even though they were painted 30,000 years ago.

PICTURES OF ANIMALS, similar to those painted on the walls, are sometimes found carved on stone slabs or bone. They may have been sketches the artists used to paint from.

IN EUROPE, the cave artists painted animals far more often than humans (hunters appear more often in later Spanish rock art). Horses, bison, deer, and mammoths are the most common animals, but woolly rhino, cave bears, and boars are also depicted.

LATER, SAHARAN rock art reflects the move from hunting and gathering to farming. Paintings dating from 6000 B.C. show domestic cattle and dogs rather than hunting scenes and wild animals.

▽ *Cave art creatures.*

horse

reindeer

ibex

auroch (wild cow)

▷ *A painted bull and horse in the Lascaux caves in southwest France. The magnificent paintings there were discovered by four boys and their dog in 1940.*

THE MYSTERY OF THE MEANING of cave paintings still remains. Some archaeologists believe cave art was involved in magical ceremonies related to hunting. This is because many images are of animals, some with spears in them, that Stone Age people hunted. Other less clear images could be male and female symbols that were linked to **fertility rites**.

▽ *A copy of a European cave painting showing commonly hunted animals.*

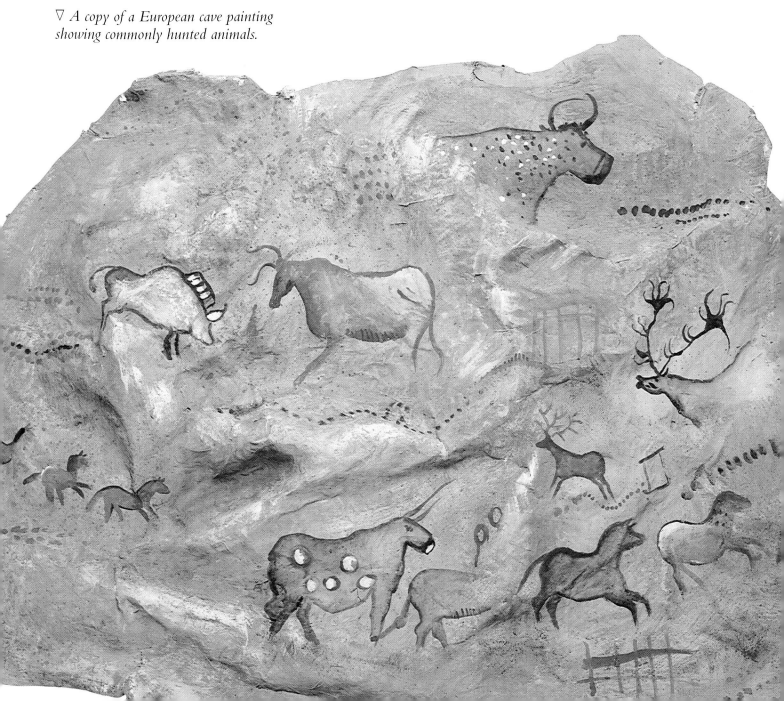

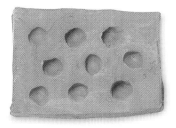

STONE WAS THE FIRST MATERIAL that our ancestors learned to make things with, as far back as two million years ago. The first carved wooden implements known are a spear from England dating from around 300,000 B.C. and a club from Kenya from about 200,000 B.C.

BONE AND IVORY were first used by hunters in Southern Europe toward the end of the last ice age. Mostly, this was for tools and weapons such as awls, spatulas, and harpoons. They also made ivory figurines of women that were often fat with exaggerated features. These are known as Venus figurines because they are thought to represent the mother goddess. Bone and ivory were used for modeling animals too.

NEOLITHIC FARMERS continued the tradition of carving by making animal-headed sickles. They also carved everyday artifacts out of bone, such as fish-hooks, needles, combs, and pendants.

△ *Some of the different designs and patterns used to decorate Stone Age pots are shown above. They include cuts, grooves, holes, strokes, and thumbprints.*

THE EARLIEST KNOWN POTTERY comes from Japan and dates back to about 10,500 B.C. The Chinese started making pots soon after. Because pottery is both heavy and breakable, it appears only where people lived in settled societies.

The first pottery vessels were made by pressing a lump of clay between thumb and fingers and gradually shaping it. People soon started making larger, stronger pots by coiling a strip of clay into a spiral to build up the walls, and then smoothing the sides. Initially, they experimented with firing their pots briefly in their ovens or in bonfires, but the first kilns appeared before 6000 B.C. in Iran.

MAKE A COIL POT

You will need: self-hardening clay, plastic knife, or spatula

1 Roll out long sausages from the clay. Coil these into a round base.

2 Now coil another sausage up from the base, smoothing the outside so that the coils merge. Repeat to build up your pot. Make a pattern around top using a knife edge.

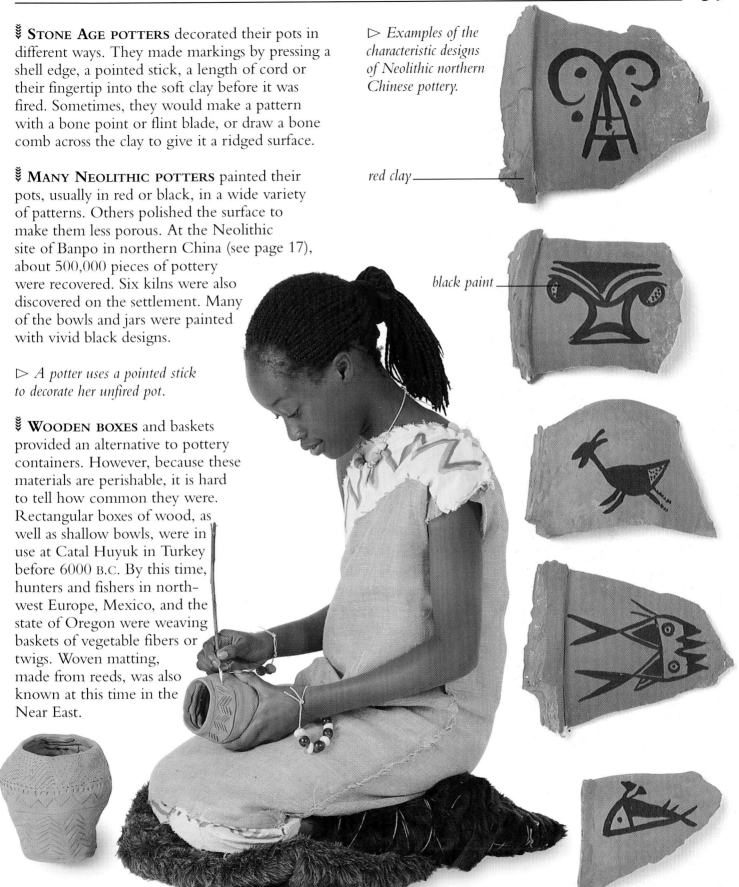

STONE AGE POTTERS decorated their pots in different ways. They made markings by pressing a shell edge, a pointed stick, a length of cord or their fingertip into the soft clay before it was fired. Sometimes, they would make a pattern with a bone point or flint blade, or draw a bone comb across the clay to give it a ridged surface.

MANY NEOLITHIC POTTERS painted their pots, usually in red or black, in a wide variety of patterns. Others polished the surface to make them less porous. At the Neolithic site of Banpo in northern China (see page 17), about 500,000 pieces of pottery were recovered. Six kilns were also discovered on the settlement. Many of the bowls and jars were painted with vivid black designs.

▷ *A potter uses a pointed stick to decorate her unfired pot.*

WOODEN BOXES and baskets provided an alternative to pottery containers. However, because these materials are perishable, it is hard to tell how common they were. Rectangular boxes of wood, as well as shallow bowls, were in use at Catal Huyuk in Turkey before 6000 B.C. By this time, hunters and fishers in north-west Europe, Mexico, and the state of Oregon were weaving baskets of vegetable fibers or twigs. Woven matting, made from reeds, was also known at this time in the Near East.

▷ *Examples of the characteristic designs of Neolithic northern Chinese pottery.*

red clay

black paint

Special occasions

The music, dancing, and feasting practiced by later Stone Age people were not purely for entertainment. People probably believed that music and dance would ensure a good hunt or a plentiful harvest. Feasting meant people could get together and individuals could gain prestige by providing the food.

🏃 **THE OLDEST MUSICAL** instrument yet found is a bone whistle of about 45,000 B.C. from Libya. Similar whistles, with just one finger hole and blowhole bored into an animal's toe bone, were used in Europe by 30,000 B.C. These could give out only a single, high-pitched sound.

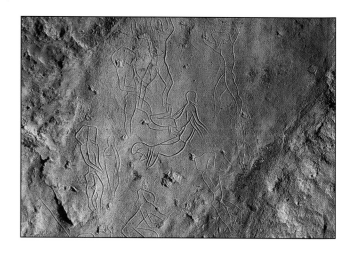

△ *This is a rock engraving from Addaura, Sicily, that dates from 9000 B.C. The swaying figures are thought to be men and women performing a ritual dance.*

〰 MAKE A GOURD RATTLE

You will need: balloon, paper strips, flour and water paste, paints, needle and twine, pasta, glue, newspaper, sandpaper, craft knife

1 Cover blown-up balloon in three layers of papier-mâché. Once dry, pop the balloon. For a stalk, roll a piece of newspaper and wrap it with papier-mâché. Glue to gourd. When dry, smooth gourd with sandpaper.

2 Paint white undercoat, dry, then paint yellow-green. Ask an adult to help you cut a curving line around the top. Remove the lid and put a scoop of pasta into the rattle. Oversew lid to the main shell, keeping stitches long and loose. Finally, pull stitches tightly to secure.

〰 MAKE A NEOLITHIC DRUM

You will need: self-hardening clay, large needle, twine, circle of cotton, paints, plastic knife, twigs

1 Make a pot as shown on page 38. Cut the twigs to make drumsticks.

2 Speckle paint on the cotton so that it looks like skin. Paint pattern around edge. Thread the needle with a long length of twine. Sew through near edge of fabric, tuck under drum and up through the fabric on the other side. Continue until skin sits tightly on drum. Knot.

✗ **RUSSIAN** archaeologists believe the oldest group of musical instruments in existence may be the painted mammoth bones found at Mezin in the Ukraine. A shoulder blade, played with an antler hammer, sounds like a drum. A hipbone could be played like a xylophone and jaw-bones could make an effective castanet. This collection of possible musical instruments dates from 15,000 B.C.

🌾 **DRUMS OF WOOD** with skin stretched across their necks were probably used by Neolithic musicians. It is thought that tall, Neolithic pots with broad necks and cordlike decoration around their shoulders may be imitations of wooden drums. Extra rhythm may have been added by rattles made out of gourds filled with gravel, dried beans, or fruit stones.

✗ 🌾 **STONE AGE MUSIC** was almost certainly created to accompany dancing. A careful study of the footprints of Paleolithic teenagers in a French cave suggests they were performing a dance. And a rock engraving on a cave wall in Addaura, Sicily, from about 9000 B.C., depicts swaying people who were probably dancing.

rattles made of gourds

decorated drum played with twig drumsticks

Understanding each other

The earliest hominids had apelike voice boxes and could not speak as we do. They must have communicated like apes and monkeys, by a combination of sounds, facial expressions, and hand gestures. Very gradually, as the human brain and skull developed, came the need and ability to speak.

✗ **HOMO SAPIENS** was the first of our ancestors with a larynx (containing the vocal chords) in a similar position to ours. So although there is no proof, experts usually agree that early humans were speaking to each other by 50,000 B.C. Some argue that the amount of knowledge that one generation was clearly passing to the next by around 250,000 B.C. must have been through speech, although it was probably very basic.

CAVE AND ROCK PAINTINGS were a way of communicating by different kinds of images, either with the spirits or with other living people. The idea of drawing pictures of a creature or an object is behind all the earliest forms of writing. But the cave artists of 20,000 B.C. went a step further when they drew the symbols archaeologists believe they used for male and female. In doing this, they created a primitive **ideogram**, where a sign represents an idea.

◁ *Painted pebbles that looked like these may have been used as counters.*

✗ **RECORDING NUMBERS** of things may have been the first written records that humans kept. From around 30,000 to 10,000 B.C., many bones from human occupation sites in Europe carry man-made marks.

✗ ⅊ These are usually in groups of dots or short straight lines. They look like tallies, where ancient man has kept a record of numbers. Around 8000 B.C. in the Pyrenees, painted pebbles may have been tallies, although the signs on these might have been magic symbols.

⅊ MAKE A PAINTED CAVE WALL

You will need: fine chicken wire, 3 x 1½ ft. (1 x 0.5 m), flour and water paste, newspaper strips, paints, diffuse tube, jelly jar, adhesive tape

1 Turn the edges of the wire under all round and work the wire to create a slightly uneven surface that resembles a rough cave wall.

2 Cover the wire with three layers of papier-mâché. Leave to dry.

3 Tape newspaper to a wall and tape the cave wall on top. Paint surface grey. Water down orange paint in a jelly jar. Ask a friend to place his/her hand on cave wall. Put diffuse tube in paint and blow out over hand to leave outline. Repeat.

✛ ❦ **PERSONAL IDENTITY** may have been expressed by cave artists when they spray-painted around their hands on cave walls. One cave in Argentina has a wall covered with hundreds of hand outlines. They are thought to have been done by horse hunters, between 9000 and 7000 B.C.

❦ **A SIMPLE CLAY OR STONE STAMP** with a distinctive design that may have been a personal mark was carried by some Neolithic people. These stamps, found in Turkey and southeast Europe, date to before 5000 B.C. Shortly after this, potters in southeast Europe began to sign pots with engraved marks and this may have led to an early written sign language seen on circular clay tablets about 4000 B.C.

△ *Spray-painted hands found in Cave of the Hands in Argentina. They are at least 9,000 years old.*

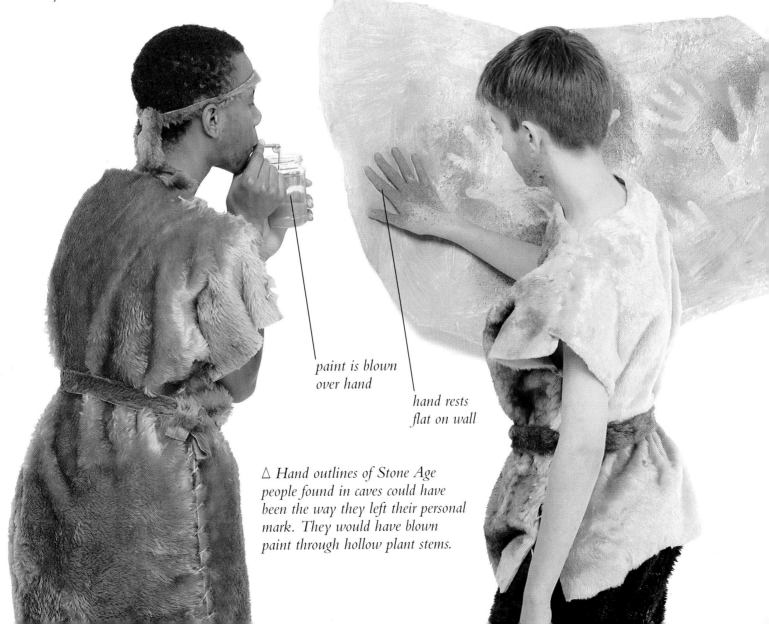

paint is blown over hand

hand rests flat on wall

△ *Hand outlines of Stone Age people found in caves could have been the way they left their personal mark. They would have blown paint through hollow plant stems.*

On the move

By 50,000 B.C. the first humans had reached Sahul—the land mass that is now New Guinea and Australia—by island-hopping from southeast Asia. At that time the sea level was much lower than it is today, but the journey would still have involved sea voyages of up to 62 miles (100 kilometers).

🏃 **SIMPLE OUTRIGGER CANOES** were probably used by these earliest seafarers. By 30,000 B.C. they were making longer crossings of over 62 miles (100 kilometers) to colonize New Britain and New Ireland (off the coast of New Guinea). For this, the outriggers had probably been fitted with a sail and a riding platform, and could carry 8 or 10 people and their essential supplies.

〰 **HOW STONE AGE BOATS** were constructed depended mainly on the raw materials available. In southern Mesopotamia (now Iraq) there were no trees, but reeds grew abundantly.

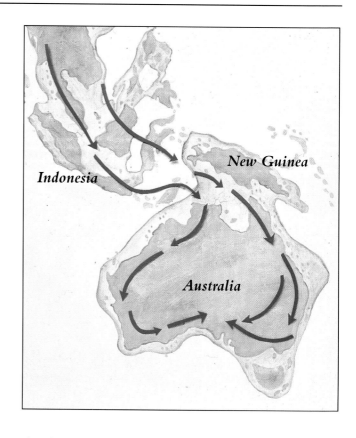

△ These are the two possible land and sea routes taken by the first humans to reach New Guinea and Australia.

△ An arctic kayak with sealskin covering over wooden frame. Seal oil was applied to make vessel waterproof.

These were gathered and tied into bundles, and the bundles then skillfully lashed together to make a boat that was basically a raft with upturned ends. By the end of the Neolithic period, similar boats in Egypt had been improved by adding a mast and a small square sail.

〰 **WOOD WAS SCARCE** in arctic North America too. So the people there used it carefully, building narrow kayaks for single fishermen and umiaks (larger boats) for groups of fishers.

Both boats were covered with sealskins sewn together and stretched over a light frame made of driftwood or whalebone. They were easy to maneuver and probably propelled with wooden paddles.

bow _____

⸙ MAKE A REED BOAT

You will need: cotton fabric, three wooden skewers, cardboard cut as shown 4¾ in. (12 cm) long, basketry cane, string, cotton, glue, paints, wool, craft knife

1 Paint the cardboard base grey. When dry, glue a piece of cane down each side. Build up sides to make three layers. Glue cane over rest of base. Tie thread around stern and bow. Glue a short cane strut across bow and stern. For the sail, paint fabric and leave to dry. Roll up a cut skewer into each end of sail and glue.

2 Paint a little glue onto sail so that it hardens when dry. Make a small hole in the middle of the top and bottom of sail. Insert a long skewer, letting sail bend slightly. Glue to the base. Tie string to the mast and connect it to the stern. Tie pieces of wool to mast and each end of the sail supports. Connect them to struts across bow and stern as shown below left.

◁ *By the end of the Neolithic, reed sailboats were being used in Egypt.*

⸙ **Dugout canoes,** made by hollowing out tree trunks, existed in Scotland, Denmark, and Scandinavia (where large trees grew) by 6000 B.C. At their largest, they were over 39 feet (12 meters) long and could carry 20 people. Wooden paddles from the same period have been found in Denmark.

⸙ **Boats with many oars,** a raised bow and stern, a deck cabin, and a single mast are seen on pottery from the Nile Valley by the end of the Stone Age. The hulls were probably still made of reeds, but with the coming of metal tools, the design of these vessels was copied to make the first boats built with planks and powered by oars.

stern

OUR REMOTE ANCESTORS tended to walk great distances as the changing seasons and climates sent them in search of food. Traveling became more demanding as they acquired belongings and had to find ways of carrying them. Once people began to settle permanently in one place, they came to rely on others who would travel to find raw materials not available locally.

PACK ANIMALS were important as there were no roads and walking with heavy loads was hard. Creatures that carried loads on their backs were domesticated later than those reared for meat. Animals all over the world were tamed for back-packing: the donkey in northeast Africa in 3500 B.C., and, 500 years later, the horse in the Ukraine and the llama in the Andes.

WOODEN SLEDS were used by hunters and farmers in northern Europe and the Ukraine. Wooden runners from long, narrow sleds that are 8,000 years old have been found in Norway. Clay models of sleds made by Ukrainian farmers around 4000 B.C. show that the runners were made from planks set on edge and small, round tree trunks. Many of these wooden sleds were probably pulled by humans, but dogs were used once a harness had been devised, perhaps by 2000 B.C.

THE FIRST WHEELED VEHICLES appeared between 3500 and 3000 B.C. They are mostly associated with people who, by that time, had acquired metal woodworking tools. But in western Europe, Neolithic farmers were using wheeled wagons by 3000 B.C. Two-wheeled carts with wheels carved from a single piece of wood are found in Holland and Denmark, and four-wheeled wagons have been discovered in Switzerland. The wheels of the Swiss vehicles are made from three separate pieces of wood held together by crosspieces.

Ancient clay models from eastern European countries such as Hungary show high-sided wagons that farmers may have used to carry large loads of hay or grain.

MAKE A WAGON CUP

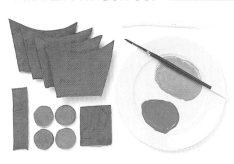

You will need: self-hardening clay, rolled out to ³⁄₁₆ in. (0.5 cm) thick, paints, plastic knife or spatula, glue

1 Cut four side sections from the clay, 2 in. (5 cm) across bottom, 4 in. (10 cm) deep and fluting out to 2¾ in. (7 cm) across top. Cut handle, ¼ x 4 in. (1.5 x 10 cm), and four wheels, ¾ in. (2 cm) in diameter.

2 When clay has hardened slightly, mark the cup sides and wheels as shown above.

3 Glue sides to base. Shape handle and glue to the cup. Leave to dry.

4 Glue the wheels to the cup. Paint the cup metallic yellow. Use orange to highlight the pattern.

◁ *A pottery wagon cup similar to this was found in a grave in Hungary dating from 4000 B.C.*

CROSSING MARSHY ground using wagons or sleds would have been difficult. In south-west England and Holland, roads or tracks built between 4000 and 3000 B.C made the task a lot easier.

◁ The South American llama was used as a pack animal and could carry heavy loads of up to 132 pounds (60 kilograms).

❧ **THE EARLIEST ROADS** were flimsy walkways of planks, pegged onto a narrow raft of wooden stakes, about 3 feet (1 meter) wide. Others were lengths of hurdle-work (interwoven branches and twigs) laid across a marshy area. The most hardy, which may have been used for cattle-driving, were made of small tree trunks laid edge to edge on a brushwood foundation.

◁ A purpose-built track makes a long trek across marshy land easier for this Stone Age man, especially as he's taking his belongings too.

cloth and hides

tree trunks laid on brushwood foundation form a solid track.

Fighting off the enemy

Once people started making weapons, they had the means of attack as well as defense. Then, as populations grew and conflict increased between groups of people competing for food and land, defended settlements began to spring up.

❧ **THE RESULT OF A BATTLE** fought in the Nile Valley about 10,000 B.C. was unearthed at Jebel Sahaba. Of 58 skeletons buried in a communal cemetery, over 20 had died violently. Fragments of spear or arrowheads were still embedded in their bones, and deep cut marks suggested that they were finished off with flint knives or axes.

❧ **MORE SOPHISTICATED WEAPONS** started to appear during the Neolithic. Danish farmers began to make superbly crafted flint daggers and impressive battle-axes. So much work was put into these that they were probably used more as status symbols than as weapons.

▽ *The late Neolithic defended settlement of Dimini in Thessaly, Greece.*

❧ **DEFENDED SETTLEMENTS** appeared in southeast Europe in the late Neolithic. They were often built on hilltops so that the inhabitants could spot attackers quickly. In Thessaly, Greece, villages such as Dimini and Sesklo were defended by stone walls. These were a deterrent more because of their complex layout and their many gates and enclosures, than because of their size.

Dimini, which was built around 4000 B.C., bears the standard features of a **fortified** village of this period, including main gates at each end and a courtyard around the main hall.

main hall with columned entrance and a central hearth inside

main courtyard

☙ **THE OLDEST BUILT DEFENSES** in the world are the stone walls built around the settlement of Jericho about 8000 B.C. These were over 6½ feet (2 meters) wide and still stand almost 13 feet (4 meters) high. In at least one place, a stronghold had been built—a huge tower over 29½ feet (9 meters) high and 33 feet (10 meters) in diameter. Later, a great ditch 28 feet (8½ meters) wide was added.

We'll never know who the potential enemy was, though some archaeologists believe that the impenetrable defenses may have been to protect against flooding rather than groups of invaders.

△ *The round tower of Jericho lies inside the settlement walls. It may have been a watchtower, built on the highest point to give the widest view.*

gate situated at one end of the settlement

Making magic

Archaeologists are convinced that Stone Age people believed in a spirit world because toward the end of the last ice age they started to deliberately bury their dead. Evidence of food, and remains of tools and weapons found in prehistoric grave sites, show that they thought these would help the dead survive in the afterlife. It also seems as if Stone Age people expressed their belief in the **supernatural** through art. They may have believed their paintings and pottery had magical powers.

△ *Copies of stone objects found in the prehistoric village of Skara Brae, Orkney. They were probably used in religious rites.*

⚑ **SOME HUMAN SKULLS** look as if they were chosen for special treatment before burial. In Jericho, burials dating from around 7000 B.C. show that skulls were often removed. Stone Age people used these to make portrait skulls by covering them with carefully molded plaster. To represent eyes, they put cowrie shells in the eye sockets. These skulls may have been a way that early people worshiped their ancestors. They may also have used them to communicate with gods, displaying and using them in rituals.

⚑ **PREHISTORIC BRAIN SURGERY** shows that Stone Age people believed in curing through magic rather than medicine. Skulls with a carefully cut hole in them have been found in western Europe. They first appear in 3000 B.C. Stone Age people may have thought that conditions such as severe headaches, epilepsy, or madness were caused by evil spirits in the head that needed to be released. Amazingly, many patients are known to have survived the horrific hole-in-the-head operation.

🏃 MAKE A REINDEER HEADDRESS

You will need: 1½ yd.(1.5 m) fur fabric (painted like deerskin), 1½ yd. (1.5 m) white felt (painted like skin), chicken wire, paper nose and eye shapes, paints, thread, newspaper, flour and water paste, masking tape, glue

1 Cut out fur fabric and felt to match shape above. Glue felt to underside of fur. Cut out ear shapes as shown. To make reindeer head, mold chicken wire to fit over your head. Fix with masking tape.

2 Tape balls of newspaper all over wire frame to make deer-shaped face. Build up nose with papier-mâché. Roll up newspaper to make two long antlers and shorter branches. Tape together. Build up with newspaper and paste. Paint when dry.

CAVE PAINTINGS in France suggest an ancient belief in hunting magic. Some show animals that have been attacked with spears. Others show men, thought to be **shamans**, wearing bison and deer masks. No one is sure what these figures mean, but perhaps Stone Age people thought that a big hunt would be more successful if they went through the ritual of painting it first.

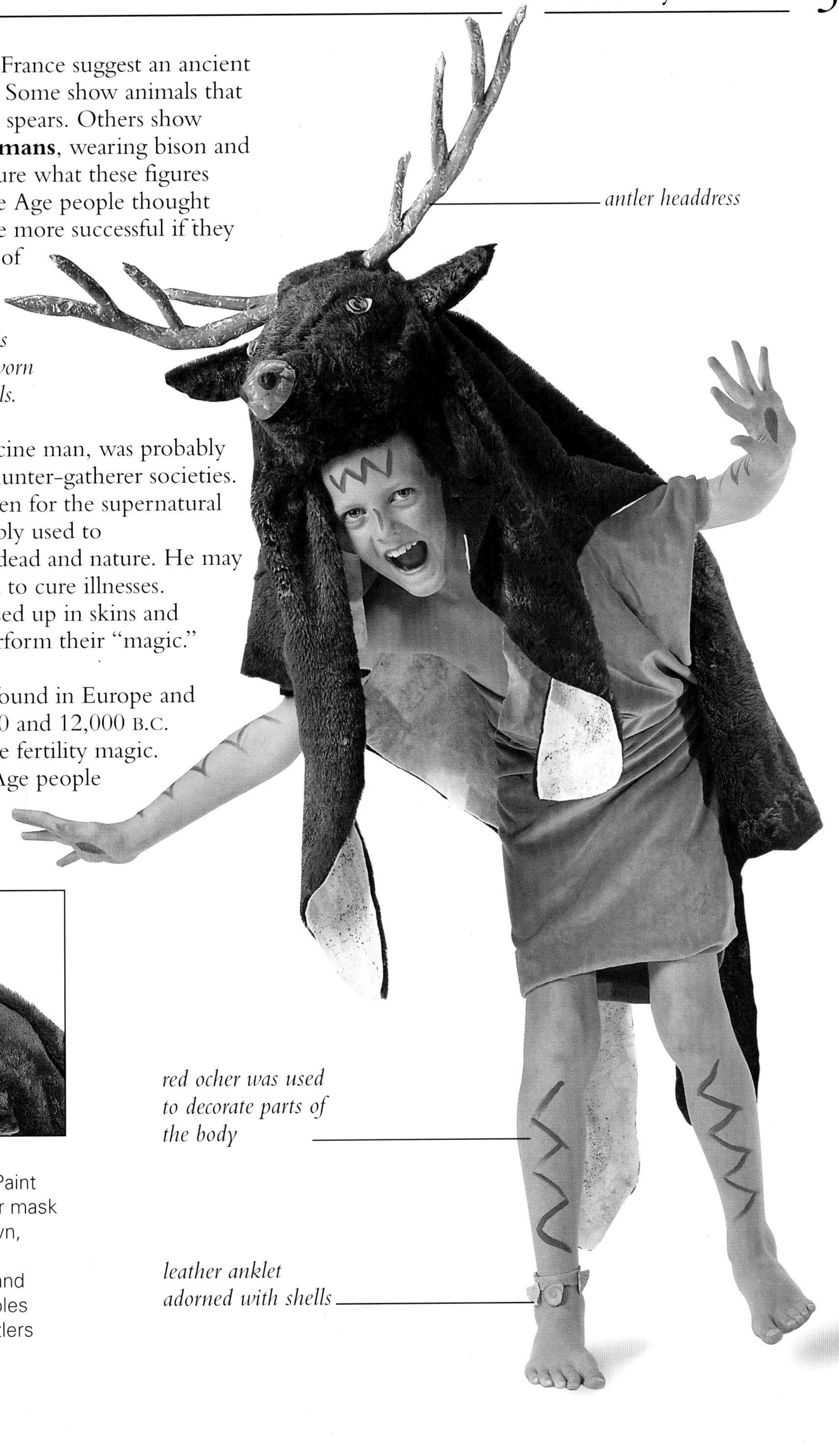
antler headdress
red ocher was used to decorate parts of the body
leather anklet adorned with shells

▷ *A dancing shaman. It is believed that antlers were worn as headdresses during rituals.*

THE SHAMAN, or medicine man, was probably an important figure in hunter-gatherer societies. He may have been chosen for the supernatural powers which he probably used to communicate with the dead and nature. He may also have been expected to cure illnesses. Shamans may have dressed up in skins and antler headdresses to perform their "magic."

VENUS FIGURINES found in Europe and dated to between 28,000 and 12,000 B.C. suggest a belief in female fertility magic. They show that Stone Age people knew how important fertility was for their survival.

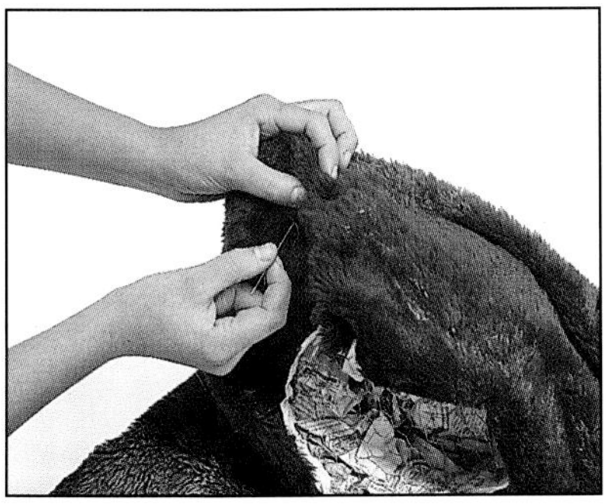

3 Fold up nose and tape. Paint nose and eyes. Fit fur over mask and sew together as shown, tucking in fabric where necessary. Glue on nose and eyes. Sew on ears. Cut holes above ears and secure antlers firmly into headdress.

THE EARLIEST SACRED PLACES known to us are the caves and rock shelters where paintings and engravings were made. But almost certainly, the first humans held special ceremonies in and around caves, trees, and rock formations. During the Neolithic, rituals started to take place near lakes and rivers, and the first purpose-built shrines and temples appear.

❧ OVER FORTY SHRINES were found in the settlement at Catal Huyuk in Turkey, each one decorated differently. Dating from around 7000 B.C., Catal Huyuk is the largest Neolithic site yet discovered (see page 17).

The most impressive features of the shrines are plastered bulls' heads, stone benches with lots of bulls' horns set into them, and wall-paintings of bulls.

RELIEF models of a fertility goddess, figurines, and paintings were also found in the shrines. The bull and the goddess were probably male and female representatives of a fertility **cult**, or special form of worship.

SOME DECORATIONS also suggest a death cult. In one shrine, pictures show vultures with human legs, thought to be priests in disguise, with a headless corpse lying nearby. In reality, it is possible that priests dressed up as vultures to perform certain rituals.

△ *The trilithons of Stonehenge are arranged around the original prehistoric henge of a ditch and a bank.*

❧ STONEHENGE in England is one of the most famous prehistoric temples. The great stone **trilithons** were erected after the end of the Stone Age in Britain, but the earliest monument at Stonehenge was built before 3000 B.C. The first **henges** were oval or circular enclosures with a high earth bank and a very deep ditch. Some henges had stone circles built inside them.

Inside these were circular timber shrines or halls believed to have been used for seasonal meetings of large groups of people.

◁ *A vulture headdress like this may have been worn in Catal Huyuk to perform death rituals.*

MAKE A SHRINE

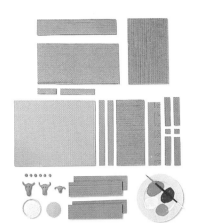

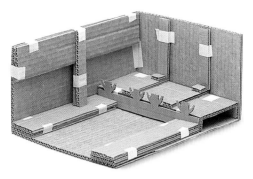

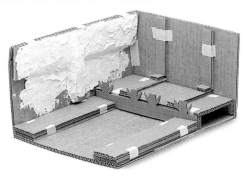

You will need: self-hardening clay, paints, double-sided adhesive tape, plaster of Paris, sand, glue, corrugated cardboard cut into: floor, 12 x 8 in. (30 x 20 cm); two walls, 12 x 6 in. (30 x 15 cm); and 8 x 6 in. (20 x 15 cm); altar top, 8 x 4 in. (20 x 10 cm); two supports, 8 x 1 in. (20 x 3 cm); bench, 8 x 2 in. (20 x 6 cm), extra corrugated cardboard for strips

1 Tape floor and walls together to make the shrine shell. Then tape altar supports to each side of altar top. Glue into corner of the shrine. Draw outline of the bulls' heads on the bench and cut around. Glue the bench to the altar front.

2 Cut out more strips of cardboard. Tape them to the shrine to act as wall supports and steps on the floor as shown above.

3 Plaster the walls roughly. Leave to dry. Make the clay bulls' heads and paint when dry. Paint walls creamy-yellow and leave to dry. Then paint on bulls and patterns copying the colors shown. Glue bulls' heads to back wall. Sprinkle sand over floor.

▽ *A decorated shrine similar to the many shrines found at Catal Huyuk in Turkey.*

painting of giant bull

plastered bull's head

plastered floor

bulls' horns set into benches

Burial beginnings

The earliest human burials were made by Neanderthal man during the last ice age, around 60,000 years ago. These were either in a dug grave or pit, or beneath a mound of earth or stones. They may have been intended both to protect the living from the spirits of the dead and to show respect to the dead.

☥ **A WELL-KNOWN NEANDERTHAL GRAVE SITE** at Shanidar Cave in Iraq shows that some of the people found there were killed by rocks falling from the roof. However, other bodies there may have been deliberately buried—ashes and food remains discovered among stones heaped over them seem to suggest this. Pollen found in the soil around one 30-year-old man came from eight varieties of early summer flowers, including hollyhocks. It could be that these were sprinkled around his body as part of the funerary rituals, though archaeologists still argue about the evidence!

△ *A Neanderthal male skeleton, about 60,000 years old, found in a deliberately dug pit in Kabara, Israel.*

☥ **A MAN AND TWO YOUNG BOYS,** buried at Sungir near Moscow, were probably highly respected people. The man was in a grave of his own and his clothes were decorated with 3,000 mammoth-ivory beads. The two children were buried with ivory spears and ornaments in a single grave just 3 yards (3 meters) away. Their clothes were decorated with over 5,000 ivory beads. All three bodies had been sprinkled with red ocher.

⚘ **PEOPLE FIRST CAMPED** at Roonka Flat Dune in Australia 18,000 years ago. But the earliest burials found there—a series of 12 graves— are thought to be 4,000 to 7,000 years old. The bodies were placed vertically in a shaft hole. Shell and bone pendants were found with them.

◁ *A body is prepared for a Neanderthal burial. The preparations are an important part of the burial ritual.*

man decorates body with powdered red ocher

body is laid out flat while ocher is applied

over the years, ocher decorations may stain bones

⚜ **OVER 1,500 NEOLITHIC BURIALS** and graves have been found at the village of Peinan on Taiwan. Here, it was common for people to bury their dead beneath the floors of their houses in rectangular graves lined with slate. The bodies were laid out with the heads to the west. Most of the adults were accompanied by personal objects.

⚜ **VILLAGE CEMETERIES** were becoming common by the end of the Neolithic period. At Tiszapolgar in Hungary, over 150 burials were laid out in rows of rectangular graves.

▷ *This Hungarian pot with a face at the top dates from 4500 B.C. This kind of pottery was buried in graves during the Neolithic period.*

Men were laid out on the right side and women on the left. They were buried with pottery vessels, tools made of flint and **obsidian**, and stone and shell beads.

In the grave of one old man, for example, there were flint blades, the jaw of a wild boar, a dog, an antler ax-head, a bone awl, various animal bones, and cups, bowls, and storage jars—probably all his own.

flowers are laid all over dead man's body

arms and legs are tucked into fetal position like an unborn baby

body lies on a bed of grasses encircled by stones

❦ **MEGALITHIC TOMBS**—tombs made of huge stone slabs—emerged in western Europe during the Neolithic, and this represents an important change in burial customs. They allowed successive burials to be carried out in a single chamber over many centuries.

❦ **AT LEAST FORTY-SIX PEOPLE WERE BURIED** in the West Kennet **long barrow,** or tomb, in southern England. It was built about 3500 B.C. The wedge-shaped mound that covers the burial chambers is over 109 yards (100 meters) long and faces east. Behind a forecourt, a passage gives access to side chambers and an end chamber.

When the last burials were made, the chambers and passage were filled with rubble. Then the forecourt was filled with boulders and a facade of **megaliths** built across the front of the tomb.

northwest burial chamber

northeast burial chamber

SOME VERY REMOTE MEGALITHIC TOMBS, such as those found in Ireland, were built by 4500 B.C., long before those in the Mediterranean.

❧ **NEWGRANGE IN IRELAND** is a spectacular circular mound over 87 yards (80 meters) in diameter. It is enclosed by 97 massive boulders, each over 3 yards (3 meters) long. Many are carved with elaborate spiral and zigzag designs. The entrance to a long passage was originally blocked by a closing slab. This passage and a chamber shaped like a cross leads to three side chambers. Each one contains a stone basin that held the cremated bones of the dead.

❧ **IN BOTH BRITTANY AND SPAIN** some of the megalithic slabs used to build the tombs were decorated with mysterious symbols. The French engravings include axes, shepherds' crooks, yokes, and boats. In contrast, the Spanish symbols often include stylized human faces.

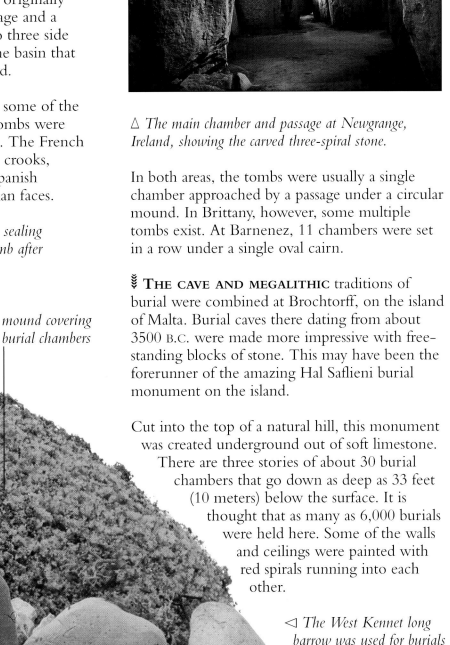

△ *The main chamber and passage at Newgrange, Ireland, showing the carved three-spiral stone.*

In both areas, the tombs were usually a single chamber approached by a passage under a circular mound. In Brittany, however, some multiple tombs exist. At Barnenez, 11 chambers were set in a row under a single oval cairn.

❧ **THE CAVE AND MEGALITHIC** traditions of burial were combined at Brochtorff, on the island of Malta. Burial caves there dating from about 3500 B.C. were made more impressive with free-standing blocks of stone. This may have been the forerunner of the amazing Hal Saflieni burial monument on the island.

Cut into the top of a natural hill, this monument was created underground out of soft limestone. There are three stories of about 30 burial chambers that go down as deep as 33 feet (10 meters) below the surface. It is thought that as many as 6,000 burials were held here. Some of the walls and ceilings were painted with red spirals running into each other.

blocking stone sealing entrance to tomb after final burial

mound covering burial chambers

◁ *The West Kennet long barrow was used for burials for over 1,000 years. The remains of 46 people have been found there.*

Digging up the past

Archaeologists spend many hours working in the open air, the laboratory, and the study to try and piece together how early people lived. Their work involves four main stages: discovering archaeological sites, recovering evidence by **excavation**, analyzing the evidence, and understanding what has been found.

THE DISCOVERY OF archaeological sites often happens by accident – they are dug up by builders or farmers. Other sites are found by studying aerial photographs that may show crops growing differently over buried features.

▷ *This illustration shows members of an excavation team on the site of a typical archaeological dig. They are led by a director who plans the dig, selects the team members, and checks that the work is carried out properly.*

ONCE A SITE IS FOUND, archaeologists may search for more remains buried in the unexcavated part of the site. A **magnetometer** is used to measure the magnetic field. It reveals certain objects, such as iron tools, which contain magnetic minerals that change the strength of the Earth's magnetic field. Other objects, such as stone walls, are free of these minerals and are less magnetic than the soil.

SMALL TROWELS are used to gradually dig away layers of soil and retrieve finds. Little brushes and teaspoons are used to recover really tiny objects.

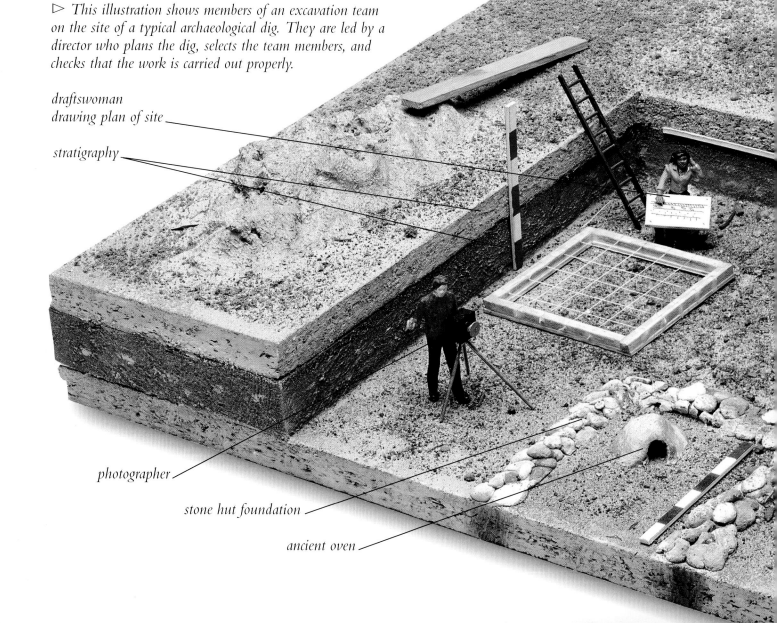

draftswoman drawing plan of site

stratigraphy

photographer

stone hut foundation

ancient oven

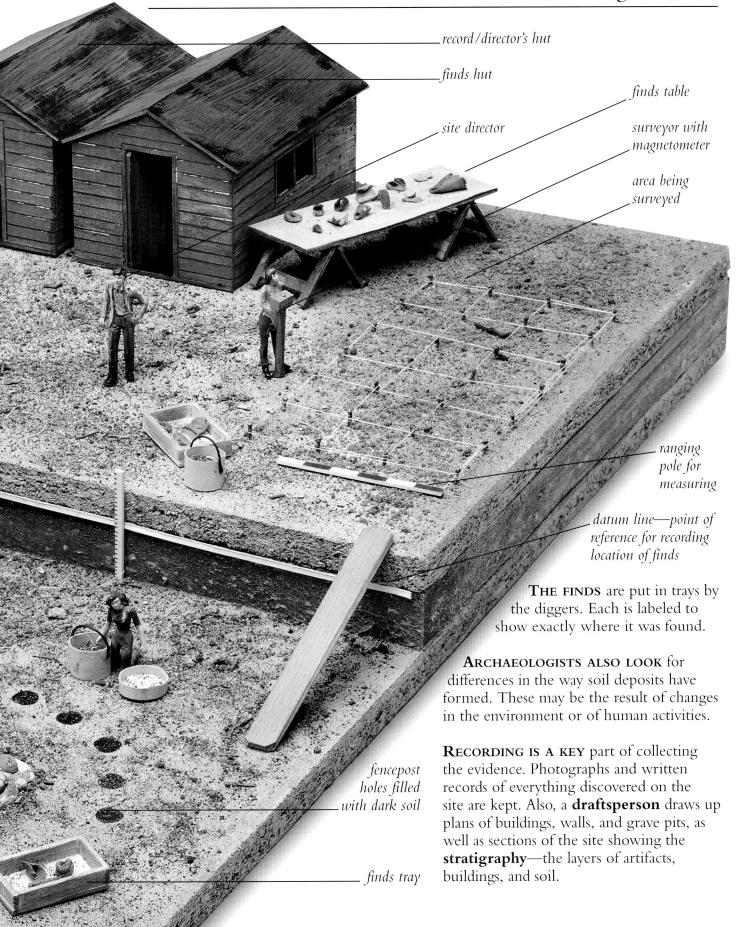

record/director's hut

finds hut

finds table

site director

surveyor with magnetometer

area being surveyed

ranging pole for measuring

datum line—point of reference for recording location of finds

fencepost holes filled with dark soil

finds tray

THE FINDS are put in trays by the diggers. Each is labeled to show exactly where it was found.

ARCHAEOLOGISTS ALSO LOOK for differences in the way soil deposits have formed. These may be the result of changes in the environment or of human activities.

RECORDING IS A KEY part of collecting the evidence. Photographs and written records of everything discovered on the site are kept. Also, a **draftsperson** draws up plans of buildings, walls, and grave pits, as well as sections of the site showing the **stratigraphy**—the layers of artifacts, buildings, and soil.

THE ARCHAEOLOGICAL LABORATORY is where all the evidence found in a dig is cleaned up and studied to extract as much information as possible from it.

CARBON 14 is one way scientists date the remote past. Carbon 14 measures the amount of radioactive carbon left in a dead organism. From this, the date a plant or animal died can be calculated. Some remains can be dated as being up to 100,000 years old.

DENDROCHRONOLOGY, or tree-ring dating, uses the annual growth rings of trees to tell us when a wooden post or timber track was built. One tree trunk may carry 6,000 years' worth of tree rings.

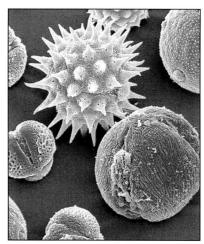

△ *Pollen grains from ancient plant remains can be identified by examination under a microscope.*

POLLEN GRAINS shed by plants and spread by the wind are preserved in buried soils. Peat bogs and very dry places are areas where plant remains survive best. Different plants have differently shaped pollen and this allows us to identify the various types of trees, shrubs, and grasses that were growing in the past. It can also tell us which plants were most dominant during any particular time.

rim sherds are the easiest pieces to sort out first

△ *The **sherds**, or pieces, of a copy of a Neolithic Chinese pot. They have been cleaned and spread out to help with the reconstruction.*

HOW A POT IS RECONSTRUCTED

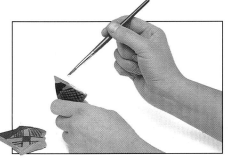

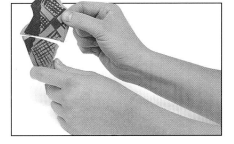

1 *A very, very thin layer of glue is carefully applied to the edge of a cleaned sherd.*

2 *Two matching sherds are stuck together gently, but firmly. Only one of the sherds has glue on it.*

3 *The reconstructed pot is supported in sand and left to dry. Masking tape strengthens the joined parts.*

PLANT REMAINS, such as seeds and roots, tell us what wild plants were collected for food and at what time of year people lived on a site. Remains of cereal grains can reveal what crops Neolithic farmers were able to grow.

ANIMAL BONES are identified to tell us what species lived in the area and what animals the Stone Age people hunted or reared for food. The age of mature farm animals, for instance, helps us to understand why the farmers were keeping them—for meat, wool, or milk.

HUMAN SKELETONS can tell us the sex and age at death of Stone Age people. We can also see if they contracted various diseases, suffered broken bones, and if their diet lacked vitamins and minerals.

POTTERY can be used as evidence of materials that communities traded in. This is because scientists can often identify the source of the small pieces of gravel they find in the clay that the pots were made from. Looking at pieces of pottery under a microscope may reveal traces of what the pots once contained and therefore what people probably used them for.

4 *Enough sherds have been recovered to allow the pot to take shape properly.*

5 *The masking tape is removed when the glue is dry. The gaps can be filled with plaster of Paris.*

Glossary

anthropologist A person who studies the culture, language, origins, and behavior of different peoples around the world.

archaeologist A person who studies the way people lived in the past by looking at remains of buildings, as well as artifacts and other evidence they left behind.

auroch A recently extinct form of wild cow with long horns, thought to be one of the ancestors of modern cattle.

Australopithecus An apelike creature—the earliest ancestor of modern humans.

awl A pointed tool with a blade used for piercing tough materials such as leather.

biological Relating to the makeup of a living organism, such as a plant or animal, and the way it functions.

bipedalism Walking upright on two feet.

Cro-Magnon An early type of modern human who lived in Europe during the late Palaeolithic period. They are named after the Cro-Magnon cave in France where their remains were first found.

cult A specific system of religious worship, usually involving certain rites and gods.

draftsperson A person who prepares detailed scale drawings of machinery, building devices, and various artifacts. These will usually be located on a plan by the draftsperson, indicating where they are situated.

excavation The unearthing of buried objects to try and discover information about the past.

extinct An animal or plant species that has died out and no longer exists.

Fertile Crescent An area of fertile land extending in a semicircle from Israel to the Persian Gulf. This was where people first started growing crops during the Neolithic period.

fertility rites Special ceremonies held in the past at certain times of the year. People believed these would help bring them good harvests and healthy children.

fortified When a place has been given a form of defense such as high walls or deep trenches.

hemp A strong-smelling Asian plant with tough fibers that are used to make canvas and rope.

henge A circular area consisting of a bank and a ditch, that often contains a circle of stones or wooden posts.

hominid Any member of the family known as *Hominidae,* which includes all humans and their apelike ancestors.

Homo erectus An extinct species of modern humans that preceded early *Homo sapiens,* appearing about 1½ million years ago. The scientific name means "upright walker."

Homo habilis An extinct species of modern humans that preceded *Homo erectus,* appearing around two million years ago. The scientific name means "handy man."

Homo sapiens The scientific name given to modern humans.

Homo sapiens neanderthalensis A form of early humans who lived in Europe. They are named after the Neander Valley in Germany where the first Neanderthal fossils were found.

hunter–gatherers Humans who move around in search of food. They hunt wild animals and gather edible plants, fruits, and nuts. It is believed that early humans lived like this.

ideogram A sign or symbol used in a written language that represents an object or an idea.

long barrow An elongated mound from the Neolithic period that usually covers one or more burial chambers.

magnetometer An instrument that measures the Earth's magnetic field and can be used to detect buried features such as ancient fireplaces and metal objects.

mastodon An extinct elephantlike mammal.

megalith A massive stone that often forms part of a prehistoric monument.

Mesolithic The period between the Paleolithic and the Neolithic which began around 12,000 years ago, but ended at different times in different places.

midden An ancient pile of garbage.

natural evolution A theory put forward by Charles Darwin. It states that nature chooses the animals and plants that, over a long period of time, change so that they can survive. Others die out, which allows new species to evolve.

Neolithic The period marked by the emergence of early farming—crop-growing and rearing animals—from 10,000 to 5,000 years ago in most parts of the world.

nomadic When a tribe or group of people move around in search of food and grazing land for their animals.

obsidian A dark, glassy volcanic rock made of hardened lava.

ocher Various natural earths containing minerals that can be used as yellow or red pigments.

Paleolithic The period of the appearance of early humans and the use of the first stone tools. It lasted from more than 3 million years to about 12,000 years ago.

prehistoric The period relating to the development of human beings before writing was invented.

shaman A priest or medicine man representing a religion that is based on a belief in good and evil spirits. The shaman is believed to be able to control these spirits.

sherd A broken piece of pottery or china.

stratigraphy The composition and study of layers of rocks and other deposits to discover their geological and human history.

supernatural Involving forces and events that are out of the ordinary and often believed to be controlled by a god.

thresh and winnow The act of separating the grain from husks and straw by first beating it and then circulating air or wind through it.

trapezoidal A four-sided structure with neither of the pairs of sides running parallel.

trilithon A structure of two upright stones with another stone placed on top.

Index